Nick Moore

NEVER

TOO

LATE

Growing Your Tree Of Prosperity

Nick Moore

Nick Moore

Never Too Late, by Nick Moore, Copyright © 2017

This book is a motivational guide written by the author as an inspiration to others as living proof that there is no situation in which any person cannot pull themselves out of, to not only live a fruitful life, but to live it more abundantly. Any references to historical events, real people, or real locales are simply points of fact that the author himself has experienced. Any resemblance to the actual events or locales or persons, living or dead, who have had similar experiences is entirely coincidental. Some names have been changed out of respect to protect the innocent and for those who desire to keep their personal business and information private.

All rights are reserved. No part of this book may be reproduced in any manner whatsoever, including Internet usage, without written permission from the publisher, except by review.

Printed in the United States of America

ISBN – 13: 978-1979099837

ISBN – 10: 1979099839

Contact Information:

athletesgoingtocollege@gmail.com

Website:

www.smalltownathletes.com

Never Too Late

Nick Moore

Growing Your Golden Tree Of Prosperity

A persons Golden Tree Of Prosperity, is a derivative of their own personal Tree Of Life. We all are seedlings from that proverbial tree, and as seedlings, our potential for greatness is already written within our DNA. What separates us, one from the other, is our ability to access that greatness gifted to us naturally, by the Tree. And then, what we choose to do with that greatness, is what determines whether or not, your tree becomes a dying tree, a green tree, or a golden tree.

A Dying tree, is one that has been choked off from its resources. Like all living things, it needs to be nurtured and fed and stimulated for growth. In terms of a tree, that would mean sunlight and water, with plenty of room to grow both its roots below, and its branches above ground. When a person is stuck in an environment that does not stimulate or feed their gifts, they are limited in their ability to grow or to exercise their natural God-given abilities. Anything that is limited, by definition, is denied the ability to live up to its full potential. And if you are not living up to your full potential, there is no way for you to access, or even recognize the full magnitude of the greatness that could have been, that should have been, YOU.

A Green Tree is one that has become acclimated to its environment. All of its needs in terms of nurturing have been met, and it has found contentment within the confines of its borders. It is healthy and is more than capable of producing fruit on par with other trees within its same caliber. It is healthy, and is considered "average," because it is no different from any other tree.

Then we have a "Golden Tree." Your Golden Tree of Prosperity is a physical manifestation of your hopes and dreams made real. It is the product of careful planning and preparation. It's soil having been enriched by your own blood, sweat and tears, years of sacrifice and

Nick Moore

struggle so that you can reach your goals by counting your accomplishments, one victory at a time. Our lives are more than the instances that we experience from day to day, for those with the vision to see and understand the power of their dreams, and the will to invest their time, effort and focus on nurturing not just the dream, but their faith in the dream, we grow to learn that our day to day struggles are not just life lessons, but building blocks, that we ultimately utilize to build and ensure the longevity of the legacy that we are so diligently laboring to complete. Success begins within the minds and the hearts of us all, but for that success to come to fruition, we have to be committed to the process, and to the work, no matter what it takes, so that we can properly map out our path, from conception to completion, and purpose ourselves, with unwavering dedication, in full knowledge of the rewards that are sure to come if we simply stay the course, and stay true to ourselves.

No matter what your individual dream may be, we all should have Golden Trees that greatly favor each other. With roots going as long and as deep as the branches are spreading high and wide. And believing in yourself, is all the seeds that you will ever need.

- Nick Moore

PROLOGUE

Broken hearted, lost dreams, anger, pain…fear, the hell that I see reflected in the eyes of the soul I'm trying to reach mirrors my own, which is why it's so easy for me to relate to him; I've been in his shoes, literally. Kenneth Henson was in the middle of a crisis. He was fighting, tooth and nail, in a silent war, desperately trying to establish his own identity; who and what he really is as a person. What it is that qualifies his worth; his worth to himself, as well as his worth to his mother and three sisters. At seventeen years old, he was the oldest child of a single mother, who was breaking her neck doing all that she could to provide for her children with very little money, bill collectors banging at the door, no food in the house, with the only thing even remotely to resemble to a father figure, was Kenneth himself, and he was just a boy trying desperately to fill the shoes of what he believed a man was supposed to be. His living situation had become so desperate that now he was ready to cross the lines of right and wrong, not because he was a bad kid or a product of the streets, but because he loved his mother and his sisters so deeply that he no longer cared about his own well-being, he would do whatever he needed to do to ease the burden on his mother's shoulders, and bring some well-deserved relief and prosperity to his household, by any means necessary. Well, in Wichita Falls, Texas, that doesn't leave a kid his age with a lot of options, at least not of the legal variety. Which is why his mother called me, begging me to reach out to him before he does something that he can't come back from, like breaking the law in some god-awful crime, or God forbid, ends up dead in the streets.

"Jessica, relax, I'm not going to let that happen."

"But he's already been gone for two days. You don't understand Nickie, he's trying to be all tough, but he really doesn't know anything about the streets. I kept that boy sheltered, safe and sound in this house so that he wouldn't end up like his father. And now, despite everything I've done to keep him out of that lifestyle, he's managed to find his way into the streets anyway," she sobbed.

I could feel her pain and completely understood the fear that she had for her child, but standing here now, looking Kenneth in his eyes, I was painfully aware that he had already crossed those lines. The light of innocence was gone, and in its place, was the cold hard familiar stare of determination. I found him outside of his school, when he should have been inside participating in class. Instead he was on the side of the building looking every bit the part of a drug dealer, waiting for his next customer. He looked up because he saw me coming towards him, no doubt he thought I was there to buy, but once he recognized who I was, he immediately dropped his head in shame.

"Good," I thought to myself. "If his conscience is still able to impact him like that just from seeing me, then I may still have a chance of talking some sense into him."

Never Too Late

I wanted to be careful not to embarrass him. Putting him on the spot would make him so defensive that I'd lose him forever. I needed him to be as agreeable as possible.

"Hey, Ken, can I talk to you for a minute?"

"Coach Moore, it's really not a good time. And I really don't see what there is to talk about. I don't mean no disrespect to you, you've been good to me, but I don't have no more time for none of that 'pie in the sky' talk. My family is suffering and I'm not gonna let that happen no more. You see where I'm at, you know what this means, so I'm done."

"So, you don't care whether or not you break your Mother's heart? You don't care about losing the love and respect of your sisters or the rest of your family?"

"What do you mean? I would never hurt my mother, I'm doing this FOR her! I love my momma!"

"I know you do son, but…"

"I'm not your son. Don't call me that."

"Ok, fair enough, but I knew your daddy, and he wouldn't want this for you either."

"You knew my father?" He looked at me in wide-eyed amazement. "I didn't know that. How come you never mentioned that before?"

"Your mother didn't want me telling you anything about your dad, for fear that you would follow in his footsteps, but from where I'm standing now, seems to me like telling you everything is exactly what you need. Maybe then you can save yourself from making the same mistakes that he did."

"Mistakes? My dad built a legacy! And I'm going to do the same thing!"

I could hear the pride and determination in his voice when he spoke those words. Every boy, in his heart of hearts, yearns for the love and approval of their father. They look to him as their confirmation and affirmation in the choices they make. The love of a father to a son is powerful indeed, but to earn your fathers respect and approval, was simply the ultimate. In Kenneth's case, and many boys like him, when dealing with an absentee father, they begin to mentally fabricate their own construct of who and what their father was. And in most instances, the image that they have constructed, is never even remotely close to the truth. Consequently, it takes the light of truth, to snap them out of that spell and bring them back to reality. That's exactly what I would be employing here with Kenneth,….the truth.

"Legacy? What kind of legacy did your father leave you?"

"Come on Coach, everyone knew my dad. He had mad respect on these streets."

I frowned at Kenneth, and made sure to over exaggerate the frown to really show my displeasure.

"Is that what you think?"

"That's what I know! My daddy was a legend."

I spun around on my heels and headed back toward my car, got in and drove directly towards Kenneth doing about 60 miles an hour. Scared the living day lights out of him.

"Get in," I said.

"What? Why?"

"Because you just proved to me that you have some stupid fairytale in your head about who your father was and how he died. I'm going to take you to the truth about your father, so that you can at the very least honor him by respecting your mother and not repeating the same mistake that he made."

"What are you talking about?"

"Get in the car and I'll show you."

He stared at me for a second.

"Do you want to know the truth about your father or not?"

"Yes, I do."

"Then get in the damn car!"

Kenneth looked to the left, then to the right, dropped his head one last time and then ran around my car to get in the passenger seat.

"Put your seat belt on."

"Yes sir," he said.

Yep, the Kenneth I knew was still in there somewhere. He hadn't been stolen from us yet. And now that I had him, I would make sure that we wouldn't lose him.

I drove to the east side of Wichita Falls. Flood Street and Bonner was the intersection to hell here. Nothing but crime, drugs, prostitution, hustling of every kind.

"Um, we shouldn't be here Coach. My mom says that it's bad down here. She's so scared of it down here, she got me scared of it, and I've never even been here before."

"You said that you wanted to build a legacy, and that you wanted to know the truth about your father, right?"

"Yes Sir."

"Well, I'm trying to help you do exactly that, but to do so, means starting you off with the truth."

We got out of the car and I walked right up to the very corner where a few of my old classmates were still selling drugs after all of these years. They saw me coming, took one look at the young man at my side and already knew what I was doing here with him. The corner cleared itself very quickly.

"Why'd everybody just take off like that coach? You got juice like that?" he laughed.

"No, not like that. It's called respect. And I'm hoping I can get you to earn their respect, as well as the respect of everyone else you know after this visit by doing the same thing I did."

"I don't get it. What are you trying to say?"

"You wanted to know about your father and the truth about this legacy you think he left behind, well, it starts here. On this corner."

"What are you talking about Coach."

"Your father and I were friends, that's how I know your mother. We all went to the same high school together. Your father, wanting to provide a better life for you and his family, found himself out here on these streets, specifically on this corner. Which is why your mother hates it so deeply, and fears it so much."

"Wait, you mean my dad use to sell drugs out here?"

"Son, he did more than just sell drugs, a lot more. And what it turned him into, scared your mother and eventually broke her heart. And that was never your father's intent. He was just tired of always being poor. Always broke. He had a vision for you, for all of his children, and he wanted to create a life that he could be proud of."

"Well, what happened? Why did he leave us? How come we still ended up poor?"

"What happened him, is the exact same thing that happens to

everyone who tries to carve fortune or fame out here as a hustler, you either go to prison or end up dead. For your father, it was the latter. Right here, on this very corner."

Kenneth's eyes were wide with disbelief and beginning to fill with tears. The ugly truth of my words were beginning to take root, which was good, but meant I only had a few minutes to twist the pain and shock of what he was learning, from hurt to hope.

"This is why your mother kept you so sheltered. Why she has always been so fearful of you being out in the streets. You are your father's son, and she doesn't want to see you die before your time, like he did. Where I'm standing now, is where they found his body. There was a drive by shooting. They don't even know if he was the intended victim or not. As far as we know, he really didn't have any enemies. A lot of hustlers occupied this corner, he simply could have been in the wrong place at the wrong time. But from your mother's point of view, as well as mine, if he had been where he was supposed to have been, which was home with his family, he would still be here today."

The tears were beginning to free fall from his eyes now. Kenneth was making no attempt at hiding what he was feeling. He looked around at the people who were still walking in close proximity, crackheads, the dealers, the poor who were feeding off of the poor, in some vain attempt to make it one more day in an existence that wasn't even worth the effort. I saw him taking it all in and I seized upon the moment.

"This is NOT what your father would have wanted for you. It goes against everything he stood for."

"How can you say that after you just told me that this is who he was?"

"No, I did not say that this is who he was; What I said, is that this is WHAT HE DID, because of his love for his family. Just like you, he ended up out here because he was thinking of something and someone other than himself. And just like you he was willing to risk it all to provide for the ones that he loves, but unlike you, he didn't have the opportunities that you have in this day and age. He did what he thought he had to do, because he really believed that he had no other options. You on the other hand, have more options than most kids your age. And I can help you. You are a talented athlete Ken, and I can help you with that. You said that you wanted to create a legacy, it starts there. With your skills and talents. From there I can help you get into a good college. With hard work and determination, we can take that into any direction you want it to go in, but there are no instant fixes to what you have going on. Yes, your family is struggling, but they will survive, and everyone will be fine. What I need you to do now, is to look toward the future. With some planning and well-placed decisions, you can put yourself in the position that you need to be in order to care for your family, but education is key. And your gift in sports could easily be your ticket in. This is what your father would have wanted."

"How do you know that?" he asked with tears still falling from his eyes.

"Because that is the hope of every parent, that their child lives a life that is greater than their own. We all want what's best for our children. You're almost a man now, the choices you make now, could easily impact the rest of your life, for either the better or the worse. You have people around you who care about you, who see your potential, like your mother, like me. Let us help you become the man that we know your father would have wanted you to become, the man that he himself never had the chance to be. That would bring his soul true peace, and your mother would no longer have to spend her nights in tears or in fear of what was going on with her only son."

My pitch was made. I could see that he was truly wrestling with it in his mind, but his heart, in the end, is what won out. He wiped his face clean and took one final look around at what use to be his father's legacy.

"Ok Coach,…take me home…and tell me what I gotta do to make this right."

The first thing I did was call his mother to let him know that he was all right and that he would be coming home and would not have to worry anymore about losing her son to the streets. We would get into details later, but now, I needed to prime his thought process in preparation for the work ahead.

He was an average student, grades fell in the range of B's and C's, so his best shot at making it into a decent college was going to be through an athletic scholarship. And that meant getting him ready.

There are so many kids like Kenneth, intelligent, warm hearted, well mannered, good souls, that are being left behind and disenfranchised because of lack of opportunity. People who live in small towns usually have to make a way to a major metropolis in order to find a better job that will afford them a better life than the one they would be trapped in, back where ever they are from. That's why I created my organization; Small Town Athletes. There is a lot that the world has to offer, but again, people in small towns don't know much outside of their own. Giving these kids the motivation to stay in school and make it through to college, is what gives them the best possible opportunity to see all of the possibilities available to them. College opens up more than just their eyes, it opens up their minds. And from there, there are no limits. They just need someone there to help encourage them along the way sometimes, that's what I'm here for. To help them employ some of the same values that we want instilled in them and their work ethic.

I take Kenneth home and his mother is waiting at the door with open arms. They embrace, and I can hear them sobbing as they simply hold each other. I give them their moment and go wait by my car. After a few minutes his mother, Jessica, comes over to speak to me.

"I don't know what to say to your right now…thank you, for bringing my baby home to me…alive."

"Don't thank me yet, we've got a lot of work to do."

"What do you mean?"

"I mean this isn't the end, it's only the beginning. If you want to ensure that he has a future, we're gonna have to get him into college. And I don't have time to half step. All I need to know is can I count on you to help me push him?"

"Of course you can," she smiled at me.

"Good, I'll be here tomorrow to get him started."

"Nickie…I know I called you for your help,…but why do you care so much about what happens with my son?"

"Because when I was his age…that was me. I was almost lost, just like he is now. And I need him to know that it's never too late. Never too late to hope, never too late to dream, never too late to be whatever it is that he wants to be, if he only believes. And in those moments when he has his own doubts, when he doesn't know what to believe himself, he'll have you and me to remind him and get him back on point. I care, because he, is ME. And this is me paying it forward.

Chapter 1

For me, the beginning, and the ending of my story both originate from the same place; my empathy for the children. When I created my organization; "Small Town Athletes," I did so to fill a void that had long been neglected in my own community, not truly realizing that the exact same problem existed in other places as well. That there was in fact a desperate need, all over the United States of America, for young people to have an outlet, and a place where they could go to feel safe, and to ask for help, whether it was with their academics, how to deal with bullies, or with pushing themselves to become better athletes. In a lot of urban and suburban areas, single parent households are growing in numbers at an alarming rate. And in the dysfunctional dynamic of the relationship shared between the parents, the child is stuck trying to figure out their place in the family, as well as in the world. For most, it's a scary time that results in a lot of children exhibiting "impulsive behavior." They begin to act out, sometimes for attention. Sometimes as a subconscious reflex because of the child's need to vent their anger, frustration, or fear. There are a number of reasons as to why children lash out as they do, but in the end, the answer to dealing with all of these issues is almost always the same: earn the child's respect, and you do that by listening to their thoughts and feelings and then begin teaching them how to focus that rage or anger or fear into an activity, or a sport, to push them to their limits and beyond, to show them that they are stronger and greater than they realized they are. That they can harness those emotions and use it as fuel to drive themselves beyond anything that they knew they were capable of. And that this is their ticket out of their small town, out of their family drama. I am a trainer, a coach, a mentor. I am a motivational speaker whose specialty is inspiring kids to push themselves to be the best possible version of themselves that they can be. And once I understood "that," my place, my purpose, and my function, everything else in my life just seemed to line itself up and fall into place.

Children learn by mimicking what they see and hear. They are born as blank slates with very little to pre-determine their views or emotional responses. In other words, they only know what we teach them. And when I say "teach them" I actually mean, what we expose them to. What a lot of parents don't realize, is that the teaching isn't just happening in the classrooms. Science teaches us that a child's greatest capacity for learning comes between the ages of birth and 13 years old. During these years the child is at his or her greatest capacity for learning and comprehending. All that is required is to expose them to a specific thing and trust in mother nature to do the rest. Their minds are like sponges, thirsty for knowledge and totally open to guidance and direction. In the absence of those things, their minds will cling to whatever else it can find to hungrily fill the void. 9 times out of 10, that turns out to be something dysfunctional and unproductive. So, presence and intent and consistency are everything when it comes to the rearing of our children.

For over two decades now, I have been speaking to children and young adults about what it takes to make it in this world. About the need for education and structure, helping to guide young minds and hearts in a positive direction so that they can excel in whatever arena they choose to enter. The world is constantly changing, constantly evolving, we need to prepare them to be able to adapt and productively make those changes right along with the rest of the world, so that no advantage is ever missed.

There are three important factors that one must always consider when focused on the success of anything;

1). Qualifications: Do you have EVERYTHING that is needed to see your endeavor completed from conception to completion? That means everything from education to certifications, licenses or permits. You need more than just "your desire" to get the job done.

2). Planning: Have you sat down and physically put your plan down on paper? Do you have it verbally drawn out to help give you a clearer mental image? Have you already done the research to learn what is required so that you can navigate the needs of your project as efficiently as possible?

3). Funding: Do you have the capital needed to achieve your goal? If not, have you already considered ways to raise it? Do you have a lending source? An investor? The ability to get a loan? Or donations?

Nick Moore

Someone willing to co-sign? Or to put up something for collateral?

These are issues that most adults fall short of, so how are we to expect our children to be armed with this knowledge? Every child WANTS TO BE A SUCCESS! Every child wants to be accepted. And to feel loved and needed and relevant. Every child wants to understand their purpose and be the best at whatever it is they love. When they have that, they are balanced, well adjusted, more focused, confident, and even tempered. When they do not have it, they are frustrated, confused, ill-tempered and impulsive. Without a specific focus for them to train upon, their imagination will use anything to fill the void. That is where parenting and mentoring becomes crucial.

One of my greatest opportunities came when I was asked to try out for the Harlem Globetrotters. Now, this had been a life-long dream of mine as a child, so when presented with the offer, I didn't hesitate in saying yes. I went into training with them and became an employee of the Globetrotters as a player for 5 months, and it was an awesome life experience, but when it came time for the Globetrotters to go on tour, they resigned some old players and ended up having fewer positions than expected. I was offered a spot playing for the opposing team that plays against the Globetrotters on tour, for a much lower salary. That was a position that I simply could not accept. I still had financial obligations that needed to be met, so I did the only thing that I could do and leave for a better opportunity, but it gave me the opportunity to work with some truly wonderful athletes; Sweet Lou Dunbar, Tex

Never Too Late

Harrison, Billie Ray Hobley and a few others. My point here in saying this, is that even when things do not go as expected, there is still always something of value that can be extracted from the experience. This same value needs to be taught to our children. When a child falls short, or fails, to them it can seem like the end of the Universe. Fear of failure, rejection, embarrassment, humiliation, are all sources of depression. And depression is a primary cause of dysfunctional behavior. When a child is depressed or sad, or angry, and they have yet to develop the coping skills that will allow them to properly express or communicate or resolve what they are going through mentally or emotionally, their instincts will force them to simply "ACT OUT" impulsively. Adults will interpret this as a child being unruly or disobedient, when in fact it is nothing more than a cry for help or attention. A desperate need to express a thought or feeling that they simply do lack the ability to express or have no outlet to release. The real gap between children and adults, isn't in the generations that separate us, or the changes in cultural idealisms, the real gap between us lies in the relationship between the young and the old, the ability to trust, the ability to communicate, the ability to be open without judgement. In the old days, the young would come to the old with their questions or concerns because they were searching for WISDOM AND DIRECTION. – Now we live in an age where the young go to each other with their questions and concerns, because what they are searching for now is ACCEPTANCE AND APPROVAL. Acceptance and approval can be more easily attained by people of your own generation, especially when neither wisdom nor direction are factors. Instant gratification. It gives the young a very strong sense of purpose and accomplishment, but there is no substance in any of it. And as adults, that is what we need to be investing back into our children again, SUBSTANCE.

There are a few topics that I speak about frequently at schools and assemblies when speaking to the children:

- ❖ The importance of listening to teachers.
- ❖ Why bullying is wrong and what to do about it.
- ❖ The need for education and staying in school.
- ❖ Pursuing your goals and dreams.
- ❖ Having the courage to NOT be a follower.
- ❖ Dealing with depression.
- ❖ Being brave enough to ask for help when needed.

We take for granted that a lot of these things are just "common sense" and really don't need to be talked about out loud, nothing could be further from the truth. These things do indeed need to be discussed and spoken out loud for them to be seeded and to take root within a child's moral compass. Ultimately, this is what I do. I ensure that the words are being spoken, and heard and digested by the children participating. And so far, the response from the kids has been amazing.

Never Too Late

My current mission is focusing on helping children to identify what their passion is. What their gift or calling may be. No matter how different we all may be, there are some common traits that remain the same throughout the human condition. Finding, understanding, pursuing and achieving your purpose in life, is the one thing that every living soul instinctively seeks to do. Our educational system is set up to ensure that at the minimum, all children will possess the necessary basic skills that will allow them to function in society, but little to no outlets exists in our educational system to help identify and then nurture the gifts, talents or passions of our youth. By encouraging them to embrace their passions and nurturing their skills, we empower them with confidence and have a better medium in which to teach them the difference between a job and a career.

- ❖ **A job:** *A means of employment necessary to generate revenue to cover the financial responsibilities of an adult.*
- ❖ **A career:** *Being paid to do a professionally, what you personally enjoy doing for free privately.*

Again, without us, "the adults" to give them very specific direction, a child's imagination will simply create something else to fill the void. This is the purpose of my organization; Small Town Athletes, and hopefully with the information found in this book, more parents will become more proactive in their efforts to help their children identify what their passions are and what their dreams are, because it's never too early to start working on making their dreams a reality.

At Small Town Athletes, our primary focus is sports. Specifically, football and basketball. I played both in high school and college. And I use these two platforms as vehicles for children to earn scholarships into College. For those who understand the correlation between the two, it is a wonderful opportunity to help develop a child's social skills, while increasing their athleticism, discipline and physical fitness. Sports is about more than just "the activity." There are a wealth of other lessons that can only serve to add to the character and disposition of our youth. Sports teaches our children:

- ❖ How to respect authority.
- ❖ How to work together as a team.
- ❖ How to place the needs of the many before the needs of self.
- ❖ Accountability.
- ❖ Self-Respect and respect for others.
- ❖ And how to obey and respect rules, laws and parameters.

These are all applicable elements of everyday life. Elements that they would find themselves using in the workplace, or in service to the community, or in service to our country. Again, everyday things that we take for granted as just good old fashioned "common sense," but more and more we see our youth turning to crime, attacking the elderly, involving themselves in illegal, unethical or unsavory activity. It would seem that "common sense" really isn't so common anymore. Which is exactly why instead of assuming that our youth already know these things, that someone somewhere must surely be communicating these things to them, when in fact they are not, I have made it my mission to do so myself. And I am encouraging every parent, every mentor, every teacher or tutor or leader to do the same. Why? Because if we do not ensure that these qualities are instilled within our youth NOW, there will be no one left to ensure that these same qualities are instilled in our youth later. In order to enjoy fruit, you must first plant a seed and nurture it to fruition. If no seed is ever planted, there can be no fruit. Each generation is responsible for the fruit of the generations after itself.

So where do we begin? Where do we start with establishing a standard for our youth to follow? We start with self. Leading by example. Not just with words, but with actions. Children mimic what they see and what they hear. So, make sure what they see and hear is positive and constructive and productive and wholesome. All of the things that a good and productive life should in fact be.

Chapter 2

In the beginning of my career I made the mistake of putting a lot of stock in the people, or groups or organizations with whom I was associated with. Growing up playing sports teaches you the power of the cohesive unit, but there is also a lot to be said about the power of self-reliance. The problem with any group or team situation is that the group or team is only as strong as its weakest link. Consequently, individual training is necessary in addition to the training done with the group or the team, for personal growth and advancement. No one wants to be the weakest link. We all want to be acknowledged as the best at what we do, at the top of our game, with the most to offer or contribute, but that does not happen without a tremendous amount or work or effort on our part. And that is the bottom line to it all, the work that it will take to get you from where you currently are, to where you truly want to be. How do we do that? How do we establish a path from where we are to where we want to be? Oddly enough, no matter what your specific desire or path may be, the method is the same for us all. And this is where I introduce you to a simple technique, that if you so choose to employ it, will change your life forever. It is called "LINEAR THINKING." It's not a new concept, nor does it require any special.

Linear thinking is defined as:

"A process of thought following known cycles, OR an established step by step progression, where a response to a step must be completed

Never Too Late

before the next step is taken."

What that means is that before any steps are taken, a plan is already "MAPPED OUT." And if you follow this plan, "STEP BY STEP" you are guaranteed to get the same results "EVERYTIME." The next step in the process is never taken until the step before it has been completed. This ensures the desired result consistently EVERYTIME.

Your blueprint to success has already been written and Beta-Tested a million times over by generations of people who got their act together by following these same principals. What they grew to understand is that having a POSITIVE ATTITUDE is key. And positive attitudes come from positive thinking. There may be a handful of privileged individuals with the right pedigree or inheritance or they are simply gifted individuals, but ultimately, we all start off evenly from the same playing field. So how or why is it that some of us seem groomed for success while others who seemingly work 3 times harder yield substandard results and bear little fruit? The answer is in their minds. Their thought process. Their focus. Their capacity for linear thinking.

Giving you the blue print for your success, (which is indeed given to you, here in this book), simply IS NOT enough. There has to be a change in your thinking and behavior. A literal transformation of the mind. And that transformation of the mind is your resolved determination to focus on the tasks at hand and not be distracted by outside or inside influences. It's just a higher form of concentration, determination and dedication. And anyone is capable of achieving it. The end result of your ability to do this will be your unwavering success in all you strive to achieve in life.

So the question you have to ask yourself NOW is; Are you ready to stop making excuses and having pity parties and do what needs to be done to transform your mind, your thought process, your attitude and your literal life for the better? Because if your answer is yes; You are now holding a step by step manual on how to experience a true transformation in every facet of your life.

Remember this point above everything else. "There are no short cuts." And in all honesty, it is better that way. Short cuts allow holes and gaps in the building of your foundation. And you neither want nor need holes in your foundation. Build it strong. Make it solid by being thorough. And you cannot do that by seeking short cuts or the quick fix. Fast answers to problems or issues are never permanent solutions. That are temporary holds that are ultimately ticking time bombs, because when they finally give out or fail, you are right back where you were before. At the beginning of a problem that you could have rectified the correct way, the first time.

As a starting point, here is a picture of what we are going to turn your mind into;

Throughout various spots in this book you will be required to say specific words and phrases; "MANTRAS," if you will. And you will be required to say them "OUT LOUD." Speaking words out loud is a powerful tool that is not utilized anywhere near as often as it should be. The power of life and death lies within the tongue. Because if we speak it, we are projecting it. Projecting our thoughts. Projecting our desires, our will. And that is the beginning of a birth. From its "CONCEPTION" within your mind, to its "INCEPTION" which is your labor to manifest it into the world outside of your thoughts. The bridge between the two, is your speaking it the literal words of your mind and heart out loud. Holding the thought within your mind or hiding it within your heart keeps it ethereal. But speaking it out loud is the beginning of its physical body outside of yourself. So, it is important that we speak our desires. Speak our thoughts. Give substance and credence to what we wish to shape our will into. Then we narrow your field of vision.

"How do we do that?"

We do that by SPEAKING life and positivity to ourselves. What I am giving you here IS NOT an exercise. And it is not optional. Read the words out loud. Think about what they mean as you read them. As you speak them. Take the words within yourself and make them your declaration. Establish to YOURSELF, for YOURSELF, once and for all, WHO and WHAT YOU really are. Let this be your set of core beliefs.

1). My life is a blank slate. And I alone possess the power, the will, the ability and authority to craft it into whatever I want it to be.

2). My circumstances are irrelevant. They don't define who I am, it's just a small patch in the history of my life that I have to journey through to get from where I am, to the future that's waiting for me on the other side.

3). I am wiser than my issues, stronger than my fears, greater than my circumstances. There is no obstacle so great that I cannot overcome it. I am determined to PROVE MYSELF, TO MYSELF, because I deserve to live the life I earn.

4). My ONLY enemy is my own mind and my own weaknesses. So the only person that I am in competition with or have anything to prove to, is MYSELF. AND I WILL NOT ALLOW MYSELF TO STAND IN MY OWN WAY.

5). There is no situation or circumstance that I cannot change, or if I have to, just walk away from to start it all over again from scratch.

6). There IS a right and a wrong to everything in life. I will always choose what's right.

7). Learn what your limits are and then push pass them. You want an extraordinary life, you have to give an extraordinary effort. What you put out into the universe is exactly what you get back… times 3.

Never Too Late

These 7 principals shall become your ***"Core Beliefs and Qualities."*** We all have different PASSIONS, but our characters should all be in harmony with each other. These basic principles speak to the character of YOU as an individual. Not what you are now,... but what we all should aspire to be. Incorporating them into your new thought process will result in some very unexpected changes. Not just in your mind and heart,... but where they count most,... in your actions.

This transformation of your mind will affect you in every area of your life. From your education to the kind of job you will be able to get. Or business that you will create. It will directly impact your love life and as well as your relationship with family members and other loved ones. And I am very aware of the fact that it sounds like I'm selling a dream too good to be true, but nothing could be farther from the truth. If anything, I am UNDERSTATING the impact that transforming your mind will have on your life.

You see, a great deal of what we respond to is based on our PERCEPTION. If we view something as a benefit to us, we don't mind making sacrifices or working harder to attain it. If we view something as a threat, we will take extra precautions to either guard against it or avoid it all together. If there is something that we desire, our minds begin instinctively to find ways to make allotments to achieve our goals. Or create a plan to put us in a position to ultimately have our way. Our PERCEPTION of a thing is what motivates us to act a specific way. A key component in learning to subdue your passions is in understanding what drives them. What you are seeking is CONTROL over yourself and the world around you, as oppose to you being a slave or a victim of your own impulsive thoughts or reactions of any given situation. The first discipline is the knowledge and mastery of SELF. That being said. It is time for us to start our journey together.

It does not matter what it is that you are looking to improve upon in your life. The material that you learn here is designed to EMPOWER you to make it so. If you are ready to make major changes in your life but don't know where to begin, this is your starting point. If you need to increase your discipline, here is where you find your focus. Unsure of where to turn to for the next step in your life, this book will reveal that answer. Because in each case, in every case, the common denominator in them all is that the answers all reside within the individual. And this book instructs you on how to transform and focus your mind so that you can access that information, access that determination. Access that direction. It will EMPOWER you to put your foot down and make DEFINITIVE CHOICES in your life. And then after you make the choices, map out the plan to get you from point "A" to point "Z." And do it successfully.

"THIS IS WHAT IT MEANS TO BE EMPOWERED."

"Let us begin, at the beginning:"

Step 1: Identifying what you are truly passionate about.

This first step, is the single most important step to your

EMPOWERMENT. It is the foundational block to which all of the other blocks are added to. It is the seed and the very core of your passion. And as such, it becomes your fuel as well as your inspiration. Oddly enough, this is where the majority of people make their biggest mistake. And why they are not EMPOWERED to see their dreams or endeavors to fruition. They failed to correctly identify what they are truly passionate about. And instead, chose what "THEY THOUGHT" they might be INTERESTED in. Or what "THEY THOUGHT" they LIKED or wanted to learn or might be interested in because of what they heard from a friend. Understand this right now about your passion:

YOUR PASSION IS NOT SOMETHING THAT YOU HAVE TO THINK ABOUT AT ALL. WE ALL POSSESS SOME TALENT OR GIFT OR SKILL OR ABILITY THAT WE ARE ALREADY BETTER THAN GOOD AT, THOUGH IT SEEMS COMPLICATED TO EVERYONE ELSE. SOMETHING, THAT WE ENJOY SO MUCH, THAT WE ARE ABLE TO DO IT WITH NO EFFORT AT ALL, THOUGH OTHERS SEEM TO STRUGGLE WITH IT. AND THERE IS ALWAYS A NATURAL SENSE OF PLEASURE AND CONTENTMENT IN DOING WHATEVER IT IS. THIS IS HOW YOU ARE ABLE TO IDENTIFY WHAT YOU ARE PASSIONATE ABOUT. YOUR PASSION BRINGS YOU JOY. NOW STOP FOR A SECOND AND THINK ABOUT WHAT THIS MAY BE TO YOU. WHAT ARE YOU TRULY "PASSIONATE" ABOUT?

This is key, because without this fundamental understanding, you will never be able to identify your passion. And incorrectly embracing something that is NOT your true passion will only result in a collapse in the foundation. To illustrate this point, here is a real life example of how this step is applied and what the real life outcome was to the individuals involved.

Robert and Ricky S, age 32, are identical twins living in Chicago, Illinois. They both are employed as car mechanics at two different shops. Robert has a true passion for what he does. Since he was a child, he was fascinated with cars. He and his brother would help their father, who was also a mechanic, constantly work on not just repairing their family car, but upgrading it. Fully customizing it from the engine, to the interior and exterior components. There was nothing about a car that either of these twin brothers do not know. And Robert enjoys it to the point of literally losing track of time. His wife, on many occasions, has had to come down to the shop to get him to stop working on a project and come home for dinner and spend time with her and their children. Robert, in his defense, insists that he is not purposely ignoring his family, he simply gets so caught up in what he's doing, building a new engine, customizing, upgrading, creating a new look, a new style, that he simply did not realize how late it was. He goes into his own zone and without him realizing it, several hours has passed by. You would think that fatigue would play a role, but Robert insists that it does not. In his own enthusiastic words, "I just get so excited when I am building or customizing a new project. It's like watching something come to life. Something that I created from scratch. I visualize a design based on my customers' needs or requests, then I draft it out and start building it. I strive to do one of a kind designs so that no two customers have the same thing. That has become my niche in the market. Originality plays a huge part in this business. But then, once I have made it to the point of actually building whatever it is I have drafted, there is an excitement about wanting to see how it all actually works. I can't finish the job fast enough. I'm ready to see it come to life NOW!" He says with a smile.

Consequently, Robert saved his earnings and invested it in himself by opening his own business. He is a bit of a visionary and both understands and appreciates his passion. His brother Ricky on the other hand, has an altogether different story.

Ricky, just like his brother, Robert, knows EVERYTHING there is to know about an automobile. His father, he and his brother, have literally gone to the junkyard for old car parts and built their family's first car. His father had him and his brother helping him under the hood since they were 6 years old. So, cars and engines were in his blood. But he didn't like the work. He hated the grease and engine oil. The smell of the exhaust. Working on engines meant staying covered in oil and grime. But the thing he hated most was the wear and tear that working on the cars put on his hands. But he made really good money as a mechanic. After high school he followed his brother in continuing their education in Mechanic School where they both became ASE Certified

Mechanics. And now, at 32 years old, he is a Master Mechanic and earns an above average living making $70K a year. He will be the first to tell you however, how much he HATES his job. Here's Ricky's take: "It's a skill that I'm grateful to have because it allows for me to provide for my family. But I don't like it. I don't enjoy myself. It steals what I feel is valuable time from the other things that I'd like to do with my life. I want to be able to spend more time with my family. Have the same kind of closeness with my son that my dad had with me. It worked for my dad because he shared what he loved with us. That's what I want for me and my son. To share what I love with him. And again, I am grateful for my job, but by no stretch of the imagination, do I love it."

This comparison is more important than you may realize. The current status of these two brothers today, is that Robert's business is thriving. While his brother Ricky, has just filed for bankruptcy and is currently looking for another job. This is important to note because it demonstrates how our feelings and attitudes toward things effect our performance, which is reflected in our output of work, which in turn effects our behavior and everything else. It is a "DOMINO EFFECT." And have you ever noticed that when this reference is used, (THE DOMINO EFFECT), that it is ALWAYS in reference to something negative? Well, like everything else in the Universe, the domino effect has two distinct ends to its spectrum. One positive and one negative. And contrary to popular belief, there is NO RULE stating that all domino effects have to be negative or destructive or end badly. As a matter of fact, in another chapter I will explain how you will utilizing the domino effect to your advantage building your way systematically to reach your goals.

Robert and Ricky, though identical twins in every way, had two different outcomes in their life's story. And that was because Robert, was EMPOWERED and propelled by his passion. That EMPOWERMENT breeds dedication and pleasure in what he does. And those were the seeds sowed that ensured his success. Ricky, on the other hand, was simply playing follow the leader. He was doing what he thought was expected of him. But it was someone else's dream. It was the passion of his father and of his brother, but never his own. So there was never that same level of dedication or of love for his craft. It was simply a skill that he had attained, but had no true love for. "HE DID NOT CORRECTLY IDENTIFY AND EMBRACE HIS TRUE PASSION." And inevitably, a foundational collapse occurred.

Your true passion as your foundational block is critical to EVERYTHIG ELSE. Because it is the core from which you will build every other supporting block and pillar in your foundation. For all of those things to be in sync at all times, you need to have established from the very beginning the correct foundational block. Which will always be your "TRUE PASSION."

So take some time, if necessary, to really think about what it is that you like. What do you enjoy? What gets you excited? Whatever it is, there is a profession in it. There is an industry that it belongs to. There is a way for you to earn a living doing what you love most. Whether it's working a job in that industry or creating a job for yourself by opening your own business, like Robert did. You can take it to the next level. Remember this:

"THERE IS NOTHING THAT YOU CANNOT DO. IF YOUR MIND CAN CONCEIVE IT, THEN YOU CAN AND WILL ACHIEVE IT! BUT DO NOT SABOTAGE YOUR EFFORTS BY TRYING TO TAKE SHORT CUTS OR COPPING OUT BECAUSE YOU ARE NOT WILLING TO TAKE THE TIME, OR PUT IN THE WORK NECESSARY TO PAY YOUR DUES TO THE THINGS THAT YOU CLAIM TO LOVE. THERE ARE NO SHORT CUTS. THIS IS WHY IDENTIFYING YOUR PASSION IS SO CRUCIAL. BEING TRULY PASSIONATE ABOUT IT WILL GIVE YOU THE STRENGTH TO ENDURE AND STICK IT OUT DURING THE TRAINING PHASES OF YOUR ENDEAVOR. IT IS ALSO WHAT ACCENTS YOUR PARTICULAR SKILL, WITH YOUR OWN PARTICULAR TRADEMARK, LOOK, OR FEEL OR SOUND. YOU ARE UNIQUELY BUILT. THAT UNIQUENESS WILL PROJECT CLEARLY INTO ANYTHING THAT YOU TRULY PUT YOUR HEART INTO. AND THAT IS WHAT BEING EMPOWERED IS ALL ABOUT."

No matter what you do in this life, anything that requires effort, equates to work. And anything that equates to work, should also equate to reward. Why not be rewarded for the work that you enjoy doing most? (If you can call the things that you enjoy doing work at all.) That is what makes this so exciting. People who are EMPOWERED by their passions, don't feel like they are ever working at all, because they are doing what they truly love, and getting paid for it. Why should you not be able to enjoy that same experience?

Do you want a life of more abundance? Are you ready to make a change in who and what you are? Are you ready to radically transform your way of thinking so that you can transform your life from what it is, into what you truly want it to be? Then the time to act, IS NOW! Stop looking backwards and worrying about yesterday. Stop worrying about mistakes that you've already made. Stop worrying about past decisions gone wrong. Stop worrying about what friends and family have to say. Stop worrying about what is expected of you by other people. Stop giving yourself excuses to put this off yet again, by deciding that the timing still isn't right.

"The timing is never right."

There will always be something else that demands your immediate attention NOW! There will always be another crisis that will require you to sacrifice so much of your time, energy and money that you cannot invest it in yourself NOW! There will always be some issue or problem or family situation that legitimately requires you to choose it over everything else NOW! Those things are a natural part of life. So they aren't going anywhere. But if you don't find the courage and strength and determination within yourself to power through those things, you are condemning yourself to stay flat footed and rooted to the very same spot in which you are standing right now.

Believe it or not, your first real step in the redemption of your life does not happen outside of yourself. It does not happen in school or at your dream job or with the man from Publishers Clearing House coming to your home to put a million-dollar check in your hand. Your first real step starts with you making the decision within your own mind that you are ready for this change and that you are ready to dedicate yourself to taking ALL OF THE STEPS NECESSARY to secure your happiness by pursuing your passion and your financial freedom for the security of your future happiness, the welfare of your family and the investment of your retirement into old age. Because ultimately, the only person that anyone knows for a fact, that they can always depend upon 100% of the time, is themselves.

There is a winner inside of you. You are a champion. You are a visionary with thoughts, feelings, ideas, gut instincts and PASSION! It's time to tap into that and to use it to EMPOWER yourself to elevate your life to the next level. And then the next level after that, and then the next level after that. And I'm going to show you how. Now that you have your starting point, it's time to start setting up the dominos.

Chapter 3

Once you have correctly identified your passion, you need to arm yourself with the correct tools to be successful in crafting out a consistently profitable living at whatever it is you do. And that always begins with EDUCATION. Even if you are already in a class by yourself in whatever it is you do, you want to "BACK UP" the legitimacy of your passion with some CREDENTIALS. That usually means an academic degree. There are also state and national certifications. It can also mean awards honoring you for your work or contributions. Anything that speaks of you in the positive concerning your ability or performance in the use of your passion is a welcomed addition.

This is about more than just bragging rights. These things legitimately substantiate your level of skill and commitment. And that is important because the more you can substantiate, the more justified you become IN THE PRICING of what you do. Most people who are truly in tune with their passion, usually turn out to be the best at what they do. Their level of commitment and dedication is so strong that the work or product that they put out is normally 5 times greater than anything that can be found in a convenience store. The quality of their work is normally much higher, and the craftsmanship is usually unique to that person alone. This work becomes their signature, which in turn evolves into their trade mark. Their own brand. Consequently, they are able to legitimately name their own price for their work or service. That includes demanding a higher salary. And rightfully so. Again, this is what sets you apart from the masses. So, step #2 in this natural progression is this:

Step 2: Physically sit down and "MAP OUT" with a pen and paper exactly what steps need to be done to secure your "PROPER QUALIFYING CREDENTIALS."

This includes your academic degree, (that means a 4-year BA/BS degree as a minimum), formal training, certifications, internships, licenses, ANYTHING that pertains to your SPECIFIC skill or ability as it applies to your passion.

Now, this research is critical. It is very important that you take the time to get "all" of the information you need about what classes or what education is needed, to justify and substantiate and secure your right to name your price and legitimize the trust that you are asking total strangers to have in you, and your ability to get the job done at the level of quality and professionalism that you are claiming to be able to produce. What that means, is that you cannot take any short cuts. There can be no putting off classes simply because some are harder than others or because they seem boring to you.

"PROCRASTINATION IS THE ENEMY OF PROGRESS!"

Never Too Late

You need to make it up in your mind NOW that you are no longer going to be a SECOND RATE ANYTHING! A second-rate producer of work. A second-rate effort at living life. A second-rate understanding is what gives a logical person his bag of excuses to always put things off until the last minute. Those second-rate choices are what keeps you in a second-rate lifestyle with second rate expectations. And that would only be because subconsciously you are too afraid of FAILURE to go "ALL OUT." Which is exactly what you should be doing in every aspect of your life; "Going all out." And there is no exception here.

You will need to itemize each individual element into groups. Organize your learning process by grouping alike things together. Be efficient with the way you utilize your time. Because those practices that you perfect in this process, once mastered, will be the same practices you will find yourself utilizing 90% of your time throughout the rest of your life. Why? Because the processes that aided you through this learning curve, if you have navigated yourself through it successfully, will have now proven itself to be tried and true to you. And our instinct is to always lean towards our own comfort zones. So be meticulous early on. And make good practices apart of your daily "standard operating procedure." (S.O.P.).

After you have determined exactly what is needed for your next evolutionary step, you will be ready to start physically doing the work of arming yourself with your new education. The biggest obstacle you will face is simply sticking it out. Staying consistent with the day in and day out endeavor of staying focused on completing your education without the distractions of every day normal life is easier said than done. But it can be done.

You are now in the stage which is commonly referred to as "PAYING YOUR DUES." And yes, it will be as hard as it sounds. But the end results are more than worth the stress and sacrifice that you will have to go through in order to attain your skills as well as your credentials. Your focus now is to stay on point. And here I want to offer you some suggestions that will help you in that respect.

The whole point of linear thinking is that each step that is taken assists in validating and supporting the next step to come. Your actions now need to function the same way. And the way you train your brain into new ways of thinking and working is to verbally recite "OUT LOUD" the things that you intend. Naturally, with all of the different interests out there, there is no way for me to customize a mantra for every single reader in this one book. So my goal is not to address the issue. My goal is to address the mind. Build that, and no matter what the issue or interest is, you will be ready and well armed to take anything head on. So grab your hammer and chisel and let's get started with shaping you into the spitting image of positivity and progress.

1). YOU CAN PUSH PASS THIS.

There are going to be moments when your brain is just going to want to shut down from complete boredom. Work assignments will seem too hard or worse, too easy. And you can think of a hundred other things that you'd rather be doing with your time. – But you won't. Why? Because you are on a mission to;

ESTABLISH A FOUNDATION THAT WILL EMPOWER YOU TO SECURE YOUR FINANCIAL FUTURE.

This is when your greatest investment is being sowed. This is the moment when you will do the most significant work of your life! Because what you establish for yourself here is what will establish you as a person, as well as a professional. And that is simply too big of a deal to drop the ball on. So, you are going to stay on top of this for as long as you need to in order to see yourself through to the glorious end of this chapter in your life. Every time you feel like copping out, every time you feel the frustration of not being where you want to be or doing what you really want to do, choose one of these MANTRAS as a tool to help reinforce your resolve to stay dedicated to your success. Repeat the MANTRA of your choice, (you can even utilize them all) and verbally repeat it out loud to yourself in a low calm voice while relaxing your breathing, a minimum of 25 times. YES, I SAID 25 TIMES. The MANTRA is as follows:

1). *"The quality of my life depends on me seeing this to the end."*

2). *"The more that I complete, the better I live and eat."*

3). *"The dues I pay tonight enhance the quality of my life."*

4). "If I want the good life, to live large and be free, then no one should be, "MY BOSS" but me! Determined and focused, being thorough is key. This is what ensures, my prosperity."

These MANTRAS, seem like simple nursery rhymes, but I can assure you that they are far more than that. These words, and other MANTRAS like them are forms of "POSITIVE REINFORCEMENT" that have been utilized for centuries by some of the most successful people in the world. Buddhist Monks and practitioners of yoga utilize MANTRAS in their meditations to help focus and train the mind to a specific purpose. It is an exercise in CONSISTENCY and it will yield remarkable results in your life, no matter who you are.

2). YOU MUST STICK TO THE PLAN.

Remember, in "Linear Thinking," the only reason you are able to guarantee the exact same results every single time in any given situation, is because of the steps within the plan. And you cannot move forward from one step to the next, until the current step has been completed. Again:

"THERE ARE NO SHORT CUTS."

This concept pertains to all of the areas of your life. That includes everything from your business to your romantic relationships. The goal should always be to ESTABLISH a firm foundation FIRST. From there,... anything is possible. The only thing you need to remember is that you need to establish for yourself, - "MENTALLY," - exactly what it is that you hope to achieve in your objective. Once you have that figured out, you can sit down and write out a plan of action that will propel you from where you are, to where you want to be in that relationship, in that work place, in that corporate structure, in your goals, in your vision. You have to be realistic about where you are, where you want to be, and about what it's going to take to get you from your current position, to your final destination. Write it down, map it out, and go after it with everything you've got. Understand this now;

"THERE ARE NO LIMITATIONS,

EXCEPT THE ONES YOU IMPOSE UPON YOURSELF."

This is one of my favorite MANTRAS because it reminds me that I am a limitless individual with limitless possibilities. It reinforces my courage and focus and destroys any yoke of doubt. Again:

"THERE ARE NO LIMITATIONS,

EXCEPT THE ONES YOU IMPOSE UPON YOURSELF."

So I'm not tired until "I decide I am tired." I haven't had enough until "I've decided I've had enough." I recognize that no one is establishing or determining my "WORK ETHIC" but me. So no one is capable of dictating my success or my failure, but me. It's called "ACCOUNTABILITY." And being responsible for what you are, and are not, able to do. This is **YOU** becoming a **SELF-MADE PERSON.**

"THIS IS YOU… BECOMING EMPOWERED."

Without a doubt, this is "NEXT LEVEL THINKING" that will require you to do "NEXT LEVEL WORK," but it will yield you those "NEXT LEVEL RESULTS" that will give you that "NEXT LEVEL LIFE" that you want and deserve.

This is what it takes to achieve what others may deem; "THE IMPOSSIBLE DREAM." And they only think that way and feel that way because they lack the drive, the desire, the passion necessary to propel themselves to be everything that they could be. As a result, they have learned to live their lives, whether they are content or not, in acceptance to however their lives have turned out.

"IF YOU WANT AN EXTRAORDINARY LIFE,

YOU NEED TO BE WILLING TO DO SOME

EXTRAORDINARY WORK."

Never Too Late

The fruits of your labor are more than just your perks for the moment. It is the product of the accumulation of all things learned and mastered and employed. The luxuries that you will be able to afford in your life is the end result of you finally being able to reap what you sow, but from the positive end of the spectrum.

Chapter 4

Throughout the course of your life you will have many different relationships. Learning how to cultivate and nurture these relationships is a very important aspect to your being as well as to your future successes. We now live in a "GLOBAL COMMUNITY." And with the establishment of "SOCIAL MEDIA" people are finding that there is virtually no one that they cannot connect with if they put forth enough effort and know the right channels to go through. Consequently, you have to be hyper vigilant about the maintenance of these relationships and their ever-changing new connections.

In the past, it was normal for a person to separate their personal life from their work place, and their work place from their practices of religion, and keep their religion separate from their social life, and their social life separate from their love life. These different areas of their lives required them or allowed them to play different roles... and in some cases, become different people. To a great degree, that is no longer the case. People continue to play their respective roles, but the social lines that once existed no longer separate people or the things that they enjoy. Consequently, we have seen great integration between the social classes based upon their common interests as oppose to their financial standing. So now a person's personal life and work place can share the same social circles. From the company softball team to the night club scene. The same applies to religious practices. It is very common now for people who meet in church or at church functions to strike new relationships with other members. That common interest shared in one aspect of their lives, leaves them open to sharing other aspects of their lives with individuals who for the most part seem to have at least this much in common with them. And from that comes new found friendships, business relationships, as well as romantic relationships.

This is what is known as "FERTILE GROUND" for anyone with an eye for opportunity. And why nurturing those relationships become so important. This is the breeding ground for "NETWORKING."

Networking is defined as;

"the exchange of information or services among individuals, groups, or institutions; specifically: the cultivation of productive relationships for employment or business."

The impact of "SOCIAL MEDIA" has altered that significantly. 25 years ago, the standard was for most business to be done in or at an office or the occasional business dinner, things were always kept formal and in a professional atmosphere. With the dawning of the internet and social media, that slowly evolved into informal gatherings at restaurants or private homes in their living rooms, any relaxed environment where someone was able to set up an upscale presentation without all the hubbub to deliver their sales pitch. That evolved straight into internet marketing with standard form agreements which evolved into franchising and others simply duplicating the process in their own attempt to start their own business. But all of that is just semantics and secondary to the bigger impact that this form of networking has had on "RELATIONSHIPS" in general. The biggest impact by far is the way that different people from different races and classes are now able to view each other and form "OTHER RELATIONSHIPS" different from their original purpose of business, based on a quick view from their bio, or a link to their Facebook, twitter or myspace account. Curiosity lures the onlooker to browse simply because the information is available. Once in, pictures reveal a completely different side to the potential business associate that may or may not be appealing, and though it may have absolutely NOTHING to do with the business at hand, it could easily play a role in the decision-making process of the person seeking your services, or products, or assistance, or expertise in whatever it is that you do. Let me give you an example;

A potential prospect is undecided about who to hire for a specific project. He has 4 strong options all with the same level of professionalism and polish in their work and their pricing is so competitive that it's too close to be a deciding factor. So the customer does a little homework by going through the bios of each potential hire to see if there is something that will make one stand out more from the rest. And in the bio of one, he discovers that the owner is a member of the same college fraternity that he is in. That settles it for him. Decision made.

Never Too Late

The point here is that in the competitive world of business, what people have now started looking for is the side of the business that makes the corporation, "HUMAN." Gives it a face, a personality. People look for what they have in common with other people. It creates a greater sense of camaraderie. The internet has taught us that despite all of our efforts to be different in our striving to be unique, that ultimately, we all still want to be connected. We want to be seen. We want to be heard. We want to be understood. We all want to be relevant and to feel accepted. Proof of that can be seen in almost every facebook or twitter account on the planet.

"How does this pertain to you?"

The seed to every good business, or organization, or event, or undertaking, you name it, "IS PEOPLE." And understanding people and relationships is the beginning to understanding "EVERYTHING ELSE."

If you are a sales person or a business owner who do you sell to? – People. If you are a person who provides a service who do you provide that service to? – People. If you are an organizer who do you rally? – People. If you are an institution or a man or woman of the cloth, who must you relate to? – People. As an educator, a motivator, a speaker, a politician; who must you connect with? – People.

People are NOT just our friends and neighbors and relatives. They are our customers, our investors, our parishioners, they are our primary source of support and sustainment in a shifting economy that has a mind of its own. They are our doctors and lawyers, realtors and construction workers. Our buyers and sellers that fuel and drive the financial life's blood of our nation. Where you stand in your relationship with "PEOPLE" will dictate the success or the failure of your business. Your reputation can make you or break you. So your personal business can easily effect your financial business. And your ability to interact, relate and translate your business to those relationships is key.

Once a year, every year, advertisers around the world, prepare what they believe to be their most powerful, compelling, eye catching, and profitable ad campaigns. And they sit on them and wait for one specific single event to launch them on. That event is "SUPER BOWL SUNDAY." And the reason advertisers are willing to wait for that day and believe so strongly in it, is because that is the one time of the year that advertisers are guaranteed to have access to the largest broadcasting audience possible. In 2013, an estimated 108.4 million viewers worldwide, viewed the SUPER BOWL on their television. And advertisers capitalized on that by over saturating the event with as many paid commercials as possible. Average cost for an ad slotted to be played during the SUPER BOWL GAME: $3 - $4 Million Dollars for a 30 second slot! For a commercial that will only be aired one time for 30 seconds to an audience of 108.4 million. This has been a long-standing tradition in advertising for quite some time. But here is the reality of the new world we live in as effected by "SOCIAL MEDIA."

Never Too Late

- As of October 2017, facebook had 2.07 BILLION active members utilizing their site every month. Twitter boasted an attractive membership of 328 million active monthly users, with tens of thousands more being added every single day.

These numbers dwarf the long-anticipated numbers awaited by professional advertisers for that special event once a year. Social Media easily supersedes that number 10 fold, not once a year, but every single day!!!

Think about what that means for a second. Instead of having access to massive numbers for advertising once a year for a ridiculous price, you can now have access to ten times that number of people all year round, for a "fraction of a fraction" of the cost of a SUPER BOWL advertisement. That is the power of Social Media today. It is real, it is relevant, it is powerful, controllable and accessible to everyone regardless of your budget. As a business person your mind may think in terms of "ADVERTISEMENTS." You would accomplish a lot more if you address your advertisements as "COMMUNICATIONS IN NEW OR POTENTIAL RELATIONSHIPS." It is more personable and again, people respond better to a more personal touch when dealing with spending their hard-earned money. They want to humanize the business and the experience. The more accepting they feel, the more comfortable they are. The more comfortable they are, the easier it is for them to spend their money with YOU. "Relationships matter." And that is what every good business wants; A strong relationship with their customers, their friends and neighbors, their family. Because that's what every customer should feel like; extended family. Customers that feel like they have been treated like family are always happy customers. And happy customers are sure to be repeat customers.

"So where exactly does this thing start?"

In the old days, before there was such a thing as advertising, businessmen relied on good old fashioned "WORD OF MOUTH." Again, with SOCIAL MEDIA being such a dominant force in today's society that is more relevant now than ever before. Being online for a lot of people has grown to amount to a new form of "LIQUID COURAGE." Meaning people will quickly say things to each other online that would normally not come up in a face to face conversation. And a shared experience, especially one that was a particularly good one or a particularly bad one, has the ability to go "VIRAL" online. Whether local, national, or worldwide! So someone's "WORD OF MOUTH" experience as translated "ONLINE" has the potential to propel you into positive reviews, record sales, free publicity, or the polar opposite, scandal. We are talking about the ability to make or break your reputation as a professional, as a business, your credibility, reliability, dependability, all of these little aspects can now be reviewed and analyzed by anyone and everyone with access to the internet. And the impact on your business or whatever it is that you do can be measured by dollars and cents. "Relationships matter." Especially in the realm of SOCIAL MEDIA where anyone can instantaneously become a critic. Via a social post on Facebook, twitter, a personal blog, even the local news stations offer cell phone apps for regular bystanders to help add to their stations news content by recording and reporting amateur video and news. No one is safe or immune to the exposure, good, bad or indifferent. So, it is very important to always be aware of your conduct for the sake of your business relationships as well as your personal relationships. Because like it or not, you will find that sooner or later, despite your best efforts, all of your various relationships will eventually begin to intertwine. Even the most unlikely individuals may in fact share a related connection. Such a network can even be mapped out in terms of linear thinking. How? Simple; it takes two individuals to make a couple. It takes a couple to establish a family. Families constitute communities. Communities make up cities. Cities are grouped into counties. Counties make up states. And those states united establish our great continent. It's an easy enough stream to follow. It takes for the first to be established before the next can exist.

Chapter 5

For as long as I can remember there has been this story about how men from all generations, from all four corners of the earth, risk life and limb to scale some impossible snowcapped mountain out in India or Asia, where this Ancient Monk supposedly awaits to answer the age-old question:

"What is the meaning of life?"

Well, I'm going to spare you that ridiculously arduous journey by answering that question for you here and now. The meaning of life is simply this:

"It is the humanitarian duty of every living soul to show love, compassion, forgiveness, kindness and empathy to all other living souls. Our purpose and meaning in this life is found within those principles. Because the end result of a life that follows those principles, is happiness. Our job is to be happy. To know love. To give and live in peace as we grow in the knowledge and wisdom gained through our life's experience. These things aid in the evolution of our spiritual well-being. And the spiritual well-being and evolution of our souls is the sole purpose to why we were put here on this earth in the first place. To grow, evolve, mature and ripen into your true spiritual identity."

- Adrian Milan

Never Too Late

"How does this information EMPOWER you?"

Simple, understanding this, will aid you in understanding yourself. And that is important in your ability to become EMPOWERED. For you to truly understand what your true passion is, what your calling in life is, you need to understand the things that really matter to you. This is about exploring, understanding and appreciating the things that make up your mental, emotional and spiritual well-being.

In our early years, everything that we learn, we learn from mimicking those around us. Our first influences are our parents. And as infants we watch them and listen to them and do our best to copy their movements, their speech patterns, their habits. And from this we learn how to walk and talk and to feed ourselves. The basics. As we evolve into our adolescent years, we begin to follow and mimic our peers as a way to fit in or to be accepted into a group. Normally it's not until our teenage years, sometime after puberty, that we begin to strike out on our own, because we are discovering that there are some things that we have interests in that the rest of our peer group isn't interested in at all. What gives us the inclination or the courage to do that? At first it may be nothing more than a passing curiosity, but if interest takes root, if you are finding pleasure, joy and contentment in whatever it is that you have discovered, then you may have well fell upon your passion. It's also important to note that you can easily have more than just one passion.

I have been asked on more than one occasion; Where is the best place to start looking when one is trying to identify what their true passion actually is? – That's easy. Ask yourself this one simple question:

"What makes you happy?"

One of the obvious components that gives a person's passion its drive, is the fact that it makes them happy, giddy, excited. It is more than just "FUN." It is an obvious and infectious joy and the source of great contentment and pleasure. If doing it makes you happy, brings you joy or pleasure, more than likely, you have found your passion. And utilizing your passion as your fuel will EMPOWER you to excel far beyond your wildest expectations. Today's society has become complacent. We have lowered our standards as well as our expectations in the events of our everyday lives. People have turned to occupying their valuable time with mindless activity to fill in the gaps of what should actually be filled with the fruits of their own labor. We have become lazy, even with our ambitions and dreams.

Now that is merely an overview taken in contrast to past generations. And it does not apply to every living soul, only a large majority. It does not have to be YOU at all. Working within the parameters of linear thinking does not prohibit you from thinking big or dreaming big! The sky is the limit. But there is a path to be either followed or completely created and blazed by "YOU." The success of your future endeavors should not be as random a process as the lottery or gambling. It can be a sure fired guaranteed win, if you simply plan, prepare and execute! The end result is you becoming more intimately familiar with your own mind, heart and spirit while mastering the control and success of your very life. Your future, is exactly that;

"YOUR FUTURE."

Stop giving up control to fate. Stop allowing your life to be cast upon the wind as though you were a fallen leaf from a tree. No clue as to where you will land or as to where you will be blown to next. God gave you the ability to think and to assess and to make determinations about things so that you can make your own decisions and govern yourself accordingly. If the Master wanted everyone to be the same, he would have created us all as identical robots. There is a reason why we all possess different skills, different tastes, different attitudes and aptitudes. There is a reason why some are drawn to the sea, and others to the sky. Why some love to travel the earth, while others are only interested in farming the earth under their feet. Some love to hunt, some love to fish and others still who are only interested in fishing for souls. The divine spark that was placed within each of us and animates our flesh is imprinted with its own distinct personality. It was created to do something very specific. And once it connects with whatever that specific thing is, everything else in your life will simply fall into place. And that includes your love life.

It is impossible to speak on the topics of "passion" and "happiness" and not speak about "LOVE." Romantic relationships are a natural part of our life's design. And for most of us it constitutes one full half of who and what we are. Extending not only to our chosen romantic mates, but to our children, friends and extended family as well. When it comes to love there are simply far too many variables to consider. And whether the bonds originate from romantic intimacy, emotional attachment, deep friendship or blood relations, they all directly impact a person's happiness and sense of self-worth, thus making them elements of what gives our lives meaning. In reference to our ability to be more EMPOWERED in all of the aspects of our lives, the impact that these elements play in our feelings and perceptions of what is and is not important to us, is too powerful to not take note of.

A huge motivator for a lot of people is their role within their family as "THE PROVIDER." This is a double-edged sword. On the one hand, there is the pressure to do what is necessary to earn as much as you possibly can NOW so that you can see to the needs of your family NOW. On the other hand, because you want your family to be able to enjoy the very best that you and life has to offer, it will provide you the motivation as fuel that you need to stay focused on your plan so that you can put yourself in the best possible position that you can be, to own your own business, and potentially be able to provide even more for your family's financial security.

If you have a spouse, a life mate, domestic partnership, or some other living arrangement where your partner is able to assist with the financial needs of the household, then obviously that is a tremendous help in itself. It's also an awesome motivator, because your mate is telling you by their actions that they love you enough and believe in you and your passion enough to hold down the household while you are doing the necessary work to cement the foundation that is needed for you to build your own brand. Support like that is priceless. And not only helps to drive you harder to complete your goal effectively and efficiently, but it strengthens your relationship as well. There is a mutual respect that is born on each side. For the mate that is helping; making the sacrifice to be the primary bread winner while the other is in school or in training, is a show of respect and support and solidarity. These are the things that families do to help propel each other from glory to glory. You're not just talking about being a family anymore, you're doing the work. – And for the person pursuing their passion; this is more incentive to make sure that your plan is rock solid, that you are crossing your "t's" and dotting your "i's," because if your fail, you're not just letting yourself down... you're letting your family down. Failure can never be an option. Quitting can never be an option. Slacking off, taking a break, a time out, deferring it until a later date… NEVER AN OPTION. This is your future. Your purpose. Your family's life's blood. Your dream. Your passion, being supported by the people who love you most. There are no excuses to make when you have love and support like that. Not to them and not to yourself.

"So, what does that mean to you in terms of being EMPOWERED, and finding your happiness?"

Being EMPOWERED is not a destination. It is the journey itself. It is the ability to recognize and to identify your passion, work out the plan to get yourself from where you are to where you want to be while doing what you love. It is paying your dues to your craft while earning the respect of your peers and the loyalty of your fans, or customers, or followers, or parishioners. It is being able to see your own growth and progress. It is being recognized for your service, or workmanship, or accomplishments. It is the lifestyle that is afforded you by its compensation. The living you are able to earn by having mastered your gifts and yourself. One element directly impacts and enables the next element. That is the entire premise to linear thinking. By establishing one step, you inherently ensure the stabilization of the next step. Each supporting the next so that you can go or grow as far as you need to go without end, safely, on firm foundation.

Now let's say for the sake of argument, that you have finally achieved your goal. And you are now "LIVING YOUR DREAM." You have established yourself, your career, your family. What is next? There were lessons that were learned by you on your journey to

Never Too Late

EMPOWER yourself that can be applied to your everyday life. The focus of this book has been on your passion, but the tools that you acquired which enabled you to achieve your goals have other applications in your life that you will find useful on more than one occasion. Unbeknownst to you, you have acquired problem solving skills. Linear thinking teaches you to be a natural "TROUBLE SHOOTER." Trouble shooting is a term used by people in the technical field to help them locate the source of a problem in a system. They are able to do this because all technical systems are simply an alternate form of linear thinking. By back tracking a problem from its symptoms, trouble shooters are able to trace the problem down to its origin. Just like in linear thinking each step exists only because of the previous step that was established before it. So the trouble shooters job is to trace each step backwards until you locate the area of the original malfunction.

In our personal lives, we will have issues or problems seem bigger than anything we can handle when in fact they are not. If you remain calm, you can utilize your newly perfected skill in every facet of your life. To include "TROUBLE SHOOTING." It's actually quite simple once you know what it is you are looking for.

Look back what it takes to establish the issue. Break it down systematically. Once you have that done, go to the end of it, which is the final symptom, the issue that is now considered "the problem," and trace it backwards. Look at each damaged piece one by one moving backwards systematically until you reach a step that is unaffected. That will leave you at the foot of the root of your problem. From there you can rebuild or re-establish whatever was broken or corrupted or damaged so that things can be restored back to normal.

You will find that there are different issues with different dynamics, different parts and reasoning's, but at the end of the day, the concept to trouble shoot them all is the same. It never changes. Everything in the universe has a beginning and an end. Everything requires a firm foundation as its base and builds from that base, systematically to establish itself. So the rule will always apply.

"Why is this important?"

Being EMPOWERED, above everything else, is about being "SELF RELIANT." There is a bigger picture here. Which of course is the whole premise of; "What is the meaning of life?" In our search to find the meaning to our own true purpose, we are forced to reflect on how our lives impact, or are made significant in the lives of others. There is a value that we place upon ourselves. On our own lives. And then there is the value that is place upon us by the people around us. By the ones that love us. By the ones that value the friendship or relationship because of our respective roles. And of course, the values placed upon us by total strangers. All of these values vary from person to person.

Chapter 6

The basic concept of this entire book is that through the process of linear thinking, any issue or obstacle can be overcome, worked through, figured out or out-right obliterated. There is no scenario that exists in which this process cannot be applied. That being said, it's time to start addressing how this effects other aspects of your life.

Being EMPOWERED is more than just establishing yourself. It is focusing on how to make it through each day of your life in a way that is positive and productive and prosperous, and to do so consistently. What you will come to realize is that in discovering and developing your passion, you have also increased your "VISION." Your ability to see the great potential in any given situation or opportunity. Because that is what linear thinking promotes;

"The natural ability to project your vision, to see a thing from its conception to its completion."

This is a mark of leadership. For one cannot lead without a vision. But being a visionary is merely one step in a list of steps. After attaining the vision, one must have the skill and ability to map it out and then see its construction through to completion. Whether it's a design, a plan to organize, a new business, a charity event or function, whatever your vision is. Again, these things, these traits all mirror the very elements and require the same steps that you utilized when you pursued your passion. They require the same dedication and follow through that you demonstrated when you EMPOWERED yourself to success. The only difference now, is that everything is made easier.

Everything naturally seems difficult when you are pursuing it for the very first time, because you are in unfamiliar territory. A lot of things are trial and error. It takes time to discover what does and what does not work for you. The upside to that experience is that it teaches you what your limits are. Gives you experience in how to wield your new-found abilities. Makes you proficient at your expertise, so that when next your find yourself in a position to employ the skills that you have attained when you became EMPOWERED, it is as natural as breathing. Nothing is forced or laborious. It is nothing more than a process. And it is a process that you enjoy. It won't matter what it is; problems, issues, events, projects, whatever the endeavor, you will approach them all the same way, analyze them the same way, and conquer them all, in the same way. The specifics are irrelevant, the steps in the process are always the same. And once that is realized, you are able to approach each new endeavor with a great deal of ease and confidence. You do not however want it to become the center of your life.

Balance in your life is necessary in order to maintain the continued success between your business, your home and your social life. Even if you have not yet started a family and you are single and can openly devote "ALL OF YOUR TIME" to your work or your passion;

"This is NOT something that you want to do."

You must make time for all of the areas of your life. This is essential for the development and maintenance of social skills and networking. New opportunities present themselves in the oddest of places these days. And a big part of how these opportunities present themselves is as a result of a budding new friendship with a person of like interest. This is important because it allows for growth. Growth in opportunity as well as vision. Anything can inspire you to new heights, but only if you have the opportunity to be exposed to it in the first place. Some of the world's greatest inspirations did not come to be while in the process of someone trying to purposely discover something new. They happened while in the midst of doing something totally unrelated. Discovered by accident or as a side effect of something that was unrelated. Some discoveries are the byproducts of a simple mistake. Just food for thought.

The bottom line here is that if you do not make yourself available and open to do other things, you are limiting your scope of vision as well as your ability to create new connections for the purposes of networking. Untapped resources happen when people are unaware that such resources or opportunities exist. And that only happens when you have neglected the balance in the other areas of your life and have limited yourself by not venturing outside of your comfort zone. This is what happens when you spend too much time and energy focused on only one aspect or issue or obstacle. You must always be aware of the needs of the entire body. And to do that, you have to maintain your balance by making time for ALL OF THE AREAS in your life;

"YOUR BUSINESS LIFE, YOUR HOME LIFE, AND YOUR SOCIAL LIFE."

This is the garden that you need to tend to on a daily basis. This is where you will be able to reap the fruits of your labor. This is where you will find your inspirations, new strengths and allies and goals. Take care of it and it will take care of you.

In the midst of all that you come to achieve, there can be no shortage of motivation to help inspire you from point to point. Being EMPOWERED is being inspired and "BECOMING" the motivation. What you must embrace is the motivational concepts themselves. Once fully embraced and understood, you will be able to clearly see how each applies to any given situation. You just need to be able to remember these ideas and concepts to keep your motivation in its proper perspective.

Courage: "Fear is the enemy of progress."

Having the vision is not enough. Having the skills is not enough. You actually have to have the conviction of your beliefs, in yourself and in what you do, to summon the courage to step out on faith and pursue your passions! Fear of the unknown, fear of failure, fear of rejection. These things have long been the enemy of not just progress, but of mankind as a whole. We cannot allow fear to hinder us in any of our endeavors.

Once you know what it is that you are called to do, it is your place and your obligation, to face it head on, with the belief and encouragement of knowing that the passion that has been place upon your heart is a part of the divine spark that makes you who and what you are. Embracing it allows for the fullness and wellbeing of your entire person; mind, heart, body and soul. That is what you are accomplishing when you pursue your passion. You are connecting with all of the elements of your being to bring you to true self-awareness, which leads you to self-fulfillment. That's just a technical way of saying finding your way to happiness. This is about "love."

"A healthy loving relationship is essential to a balanced and prosperous lifestyle."

Because now that you possess the knowledge and skills capable of enabling you to pursue, attain and live your passion as a full-fledged career and not just a dream, it's important to maintain "WHY" you are doing so. And that will always come back to "LOVE." The love of family and the love of what you do. The human condition is nothing more than a vessel of flesh that acts out the impulses and desires of the mind, the heart and the soul. Our physical bodies have cravings that our lower selves, or instincts, seek to satisfy and our higher selves seek to put meaning and order to. This is the drive and the essence of our entire civilization. Our need to feed our desires. Some desires are NOBLE ones and the manifestation or achievement of them becomes something that can be shared with the world. Inventions, advances in science, higher levels of education, understanding and communing with self, with each other, with God. Some are purely self-serving, our sex drives. Our appetites for food or fun or other various pleasures of the flesh. How you cultivate and control it will impact how it effects or controls you. Preferably, you want to be the one in control of your impulses, and not the other way around.

Networking Vs. Sharing: Knowing the difference.

In a lot of ways these two are similar with one major difference: In "NETWORKING" it is always the intention to create relationships specifically for sharing information or favors for the purpose of future profit or gain. You are attempting to plant a seed with the hope of it reaping you some future benefit or advantage that will ultimately equate to financial gain. Giving "tit" will earn you "tat", so to speak.

In "SHARING" you are giving of your own free will, out of the goodness of your heart, with no expectation of receiving anything back in return. Reciprocation is not necessary. Both acts have the capacity or the ability to actually yield the same results. And in some cases, depending on who you are dealing with, the kindness of sharing as oppose to networking can yield you even greater rewards. For the purposes of business and family, it is important to know the difference between the two and to NOT confuse them. There is a reason why "FAMILY" is kept separate from "BUSINESS." The two are rarely conducive to each other. That does not mean that it is impossible to do, simply that you need to be extra careful that the lines of communication are clear, and that BUSINESS remains BUSINESS. And does not become transformed into something else. Family and friends have a tendency to FEEL LIKE they are due special privileges because of your relationship. So, they look for freebies, money, passes on debts or consider your kindness as a favor that never needed to be paid back in the first place. And from those misunderstandings comes bad blood. No one likes to feel like they are being taken advantage of. Friends, brothers, family have become enemies over not knowing the difference between business, sharing, networking, and what is expected of each other in general. "COMMUNICATION" is the answer to all of that. Establish and know the rules BEFORE anything ever changes hands. Everything else should be business as usual.

Communication: "The greatest tool you will ever possess."

From the conception of an idea all the way through until you have managed to bring it into physical manifestation, nothing is more important than your ability to communicate your thoughts, your feelings, your intentions, your passions or your vision, to others. Effective communication is what is needed when trying to persuade someone over to your way of thinking or seeing things. Effective communication bridges the gap between misunderstandings and the truth. It is a powerful tool in negotiations of any kind and the universal answer to erasing all confusion regardless to what it pertains to.

I did not set out in my life to become a writer. I became a motivational speaker first because I realized the power that words possess if utilized correctly and efficiently. So, I became a "WORDSMITH." Later I realized that I could reach considerably more people if I were to have my words published. That is how and why I became a writer. Men and women come and go, meaning that we are born, but eventually we must all die, but their words can still live on. The lessons that we have to teach, the passions that we have to share, the thoughts and feelings and ideas that we possess, these things are timeless. Think about it, the father of modern day psychology is a man by the name of Sigmund Freud. Every accredited college on the planet teaches Psychology as a Major with his book as the primary source for their curriculum. His thoughts, his ideas, his beliefs. Sigmund Freud died on September 23, 1939, at age 83, but the entire planet acknowledges his genius as relevant even today. Even if you actually don't agree with some of his conclusions or interpretations of things, the bottom line is that you cannot get your degree in Psychology without passing "HIS" course.

Albert Einstein, who was told as a child that he would be a failure and never amount to much, was one of the greatest human minds in the history of our entire human civilization. This man, who was a lover of peace and of family, became so concise in his ability to communicate, that he was able to teach us a whole new dimension in understanding numbers and their power as applied to physics, meta-physics, and science. From him came the harnessing of the atom and nuclear power. No one in history has contributed more scientifically, oddly enough, that was never even his intention. And do you realize that William Shakespeare, who died on April 23, 1616, is still the authority on all things theatric? His work is still the standard in which a great deal of the industry still strives to attain. Homer who died in the 8th century B.C. is the author of "The Odyssey, and "Iliad" is considered the "GREATEST GREEK POET OF ALL TIME. PERIOD." Hollywood still makes movies from his writings. My point here is that by mastering your ability to truly communicate effectively and efficiently, what you do has the power to not only have an impact now...but for years to come... for generations to come.

Now in terms of relationships, communication can take on a whole different meaning. It's important to understand, and to not beat around the bush about it. So here it is:

After you have paid your dues and earned your skills and abilities and all of the bounty that comes from the hard work that you have put into pursuing your passion, you will find that you will develop a very low tolerance for procrastinators, fakers, laziness, non-sense and people who regularly make excuses instead of getting things done. You will find that pursuing your passion has given you a much clearer vision and understanding of the world around you. And in the midst of the life that you've made for yourself, the family that you've made for yourself, the home that you've made for yourself, you will want to protect it and them by keeping all of those negative elements and negative people away from you and yours.

A classic long-standing mistake that is still being made by millions of people today, is the allowing of any and all "TOXIC RELATIONSHIPS" into their personal space. We all have friends or family members who we have grown up with who just never seem to mature or wise up. They are always coming up short. Always needy. And always have something negative to say or to contribute about someone else, while allowing their own life to be a burden upon someone else. (The pot calling the kettle black, so to speak). Some sense of loyalty keeps a door open that allows them to still be a part of your life. Sometimes when people have been with you for so long, you just feel obligated to always take up the slack where they are concerned, or always make an exception for them and their behavior, or lack of input, or funds, or contribution. As a friend, as a family member, one should always be able to be flexible where they are concerned; Right?

"WRONG!"

The same applies to friends or family members and even co-workers with whom you cannot have a civil conversation with. We all know that person who always has to say the opposite of what you are saying and is dead set on always having the last word. It's not even about right or wrong. It's just to spite you. We call them "HATERS." And that brings me to an old adage that I want to officially dispel here and now. Have you ever heard the old cliché;

"Keep your friends close, but keep your enemies closer."

This is idiocy. Ignorance only begets ignorance. Utilizing your new found prowess in linear thinking, is there any form of logic that suggests that allowing negativity of ANY KIND into your circle is beneficial in any way? The answer to that is a resounding NO. And that is why you need to make it up in your mind that you will NOT allow people of that nature into your circle of trust or productivity. The only thing that they can contribute is distraction, frustration, anxiety, stress, and emotional unrest. Cut them out of your life. It's just that simple. As a responsible adult you have to come to a point where you need to decide for yourself the kinds of people that you are going to allow to continue to be in your circle.

Now, that does not mean to cut off anyone who does not agree with everything you say. You will not always be right. And everyone has a right to their own individual thoughts, feelings and opinions about any given subject. The bottom line is that different people think differently and for different reasons. And that's ok. Not everyone has the ability to think things through the way you have been taught to. And it's always good to have another perspective or point of view for any situation. Just take the time to know the difference between a "difference of opinion," and a hater. And then treat it accordingly.

This is the point in my writings where my book goes from being rhetorical and conceptual, to being "literal." It doesn't matter if you are new to the concept of linear thinking or if you have mastered it, the one thing that everyone needs to be able to grasp and execute without question or fail, is their ability to communicate. Communicating your thoughts, your feelings, your wants or needs, is paramount and essential to the cohesion of every other aspect of your life. Your ability to do this effectively can actually determine how far you are able to progress and succeed in any endeavor.

Chapter 7

As a rule, you need to know, understand and fully believe that nothing has more influence over you, than "YOU" do. And that anything that affects you, whether it is from outside of you, or from within yourself, is within your ability to control.

Sometimes we turn away from the things that we love or care about the most because of "FEAR." Fear of failure. Fear of rejection. Fear of not being good enough or strong enough, smart enough or good looking enough. Fear of falling short. Fear of not performing. Fear of letting others down. The only thing that we actually should be afraid of, is the lost opportunity that we are creating by trying to ignore the precious gift of the passion God put in us all in the first place. Whether it is for a loved one, a cause, a goal or a lifelong dream, your ambitions, your visions of all of the possibilities of what you could be,... that you should be,... that you would be,... If you only make a stand and resolve it in your mind now to have some faith and take a chance. The calling on your life, this passion that drives you to no end, it was placed upon your heart for a reason. Don't ignore it or hide from it because of fear. Embrace it and allow it to motivate you to boldly step forth in confidence to claim the thing that you know you were made to do.

Anything that begins to manifest itself as an obstacle to you, prohibiting you from further progress, is only an obstacle if you choose to do NOTHING about it. Particularly an obstacle like "FEAR." More than 75% of our fears manifest out of NOT KNOWING what the outcome will be. Our temperaments are naturally fearful of negative outcomes or impacts. And that fear is what keeps us from venturing forward into steady progression which eventuates into the achievement of your goals, which equates to the achievement of your prosperity.

You don't have to be a slave to those fears. Everyone has the potential to do a great deal more than they are currently doing. The only reason they are not, is because a great many people limit themselves and the scope of their vision as well as their passion because of their need to stay in the safety of their "COMFORT ZONES." And there is nothing wrong with that. For some, that is more than enough. Their lives are already comfortable therefore making it unreasonable to do anything that would change, alter, or jeopardize the comfort level that they have already achieved. Mostly it's a life rooted in the normalcy and consistency of a steady routine that never changes. For others, like myself, we want to see and feel and experience the fullness of everything that life has to offer. We want to explore our full potential. See our dreams, our visions, our passions come to fruition. Now that doesn't mean that we don't live within the confines of some kind of structure. Just like everyone else, we have responsibilities that have to be met. Bills that have to be paid. Loved ones to care for. Spouses, children. So our responsibilities have not been abandoned. But we MAKE THE TIME, make the provisions necessary to accommodate the facilitation of the things we want to do, or to achieve. Because we know and understand that these things will not happen by themselves.

Conquering fear as an obstacle in your life is a simple matter. As long as we are not talking about something with an overwhelming possibility of doing you great bodily harm or causing you death, it's a simple process of employing the tools of linear thinking. Which works like this:

1). Weigh the Pros and Cons:

Identify all of the issues that go against you doing what you want to do.

2). Then legitimize how to eliminate them.

For example, if one of the things that poses an obstacle against you pursuing an endeavor is "finances," determine what it would take for you to get what you need so that finances would no longer be a negative factor. Once that is done, "finances" are no longer listed as a Con. You can do that for every issue that you have listed on the Con side. Once you have eliminated every issue on the Con side, you no longer have a legitimate fear as an obstacle in opposition to you striving toward your endeavor.

Now, this will work for any scenario except for one. And that scenario is if the fear that you have holding you back, is not something tangible like finances, or lack of equipment, or additional members of a team that require the extra man power. If the fear that is holding you back is "PSYCHOLOGICAL," meaning there is nothing that can be listed on the Con side. It's just good old fashioned plain "FEAR," for example, you have always had a desire to go sky diving. It looks fun, all of your friends enjoy it, but you have a natural fear of heights that you have never been able to overcome, then what you need is meditative training. Because that too is a fear that can be overcome. Nothing is beyond your ability to change. – Nothing.

"You are the author of your own life.

You can write your life's story any way that you please,

To make it anything that you want it to be.

All you have to do is start writing it,

By starting to live it!

It's never too late to start a new beginning,

And it's never too late to start over from an old ending."

Most people have conditioned their minds to believe that if they have not accomplished a deed or a task in their lives before a certain time period that they have missed or lost the opportunity to every achieve it, or experience it. This is a commonly misunderstood and false statement that has been generally accepted as the truth.

There is no such thing as "TOO LATE." As long as you still have breath in your body and life in your limbs, if you have a desire in your heart to do something, to see something, to experience something, the only thing that is stopping you... is "YOU."

A person can live an entire lifetime doing what they need to do to survive and being completely miserable doing so, but they endure in order to meet their responsibilities. For many of us, life is a struggle. My logic however is fairly simple. If your life is going to be a struggle anyway, why not let it be a struggle while doing the things that you actually WANT TO BE DOING?

If you know that you are unhappy in your life anyway, please know that at any time that you deem yourself ready, that you can literally STOP whatever it is that you are doing and begin living your life in pursuit of the things that make you happy. Your age is never an obstacle or an issue. If you want it bad enough, all you have to do is roll up your sleeves and make it up in your mind that you are ready to do the work necessary to make it happen.

The trick to actually pursuing your dreams is simply to start becoming active in whatever your particular dream is. Meaning you need to PHYSICALLY be doing whatever your particular passion is. Start off small if you don't really have experience in it. Take a class in it. Work up under someone who is skilled in it. Become an apprentice. Become someone's intern. There is always a way for you to take the baby steps you need as an entry way into the world that you want to be a part of. But you have to physically take the steps for it to be real. Keeping your dreams, your vision, your passion pent up inside of yourself can become toxic. It can actually make a person bitter. Because there will always be that longing to do this thing that your soul is longing to do. And never being able to answer that call or pursue those ambitions can force a person to feel as though they have wasted their life. Because they feel,...they know, deep down in their heart of hearts that they were put here on this earth to do more than what they have come to do.

Your life can begin at age 29. Or at age 54. You can begin a brand new life and a brand new adventure at age 75! You are as young as you believe you are. And your life can be as full as you want it to be. There are no limits except the ones that we place on ourselves.

"Sometimes we forget that we were not always as smart or as blessed as we are now, but we are quick to try and hold the next person up to our standards. That is not being realistic at all. You have to be ACCEPTING of who and what a person is at THIS POINT IN THEIR LIVES. Everyone is NOT en sync with the same evolutionary clock that you are. So be patient and kind with those you interact with. Some will be wiser, some will be slower, but all are deserving of your RESPECT."

It's important that we do not alienate the people in our lives that we love. If you are reading this book, then clearly you are a person who seeks to improve or better themselves by adding to your knowledge base, the wisdom and expertise of others. A wise person knows that there is always something more to learn. Always something more to add, that will help enhance the quality of their life. And as you accumulate those lessons and life experiences, you raise both your intelligence and your consciousness. That is one of the benefits to enrichening your spirit with the things that add onto your life as a whole. And it is not easily earned. It comes only after investing the time and energy it took for you to live and experience the life that you have thus far. A friend or family member who has NOT partook in a similar journey or shared similar experiences, simply cannot relate. They will not have the same appreciation for things you speak of, because only YOU lived it. They can only theorize about. You will have a very passionate opinionated feeling about it. They will be indifferent about it, because they do not have a firsthand experience to relate it to.

Here is where you want to be mindful. People in long term friendships have ended those friendships because they felt as though their friends were no longer of the same ilk. That they have outgrown them. And on rare occasions that can happen, but mostly that is not the case.

Know the difference between outgrowing a relationship and simply becoming arrogant. Now, it is indeed possible for a person to grow so much within his own personal development that they outgrow their current circle of friends. Particularly if they are young. A lot of who we are becomes defined by "WHAT WE DO." So, if your interests change and you find yourself doing new things that your circle are not interested in doing, then there is a natural gravitating away from each other as your interest deepens and you begin spending more and more time doing what you love. That is different from not wanting to socialize with someone because "NOW" you feel as though they are beneath you. If that is indeed the case, then you need to seriously re-evaluate "YOURSELF." And what is it about "YOU" that has changed. Why were they good enough to be a genuine friend before, but not now? Self-checks help to keep us grounded. There is nothing wrong with always wanting to reach for the stars, just remember that everything that goes up, eventually has to come back down. And that whatever you have left behind, will still be there waiting for you when you get back.

You want to always remember that a humble heart allows for us to be accepting of one another as we are. And to not place demands or expectations unfairly on others. The same way you had the right to expand your horizons, likewise, they have the same right to be perfectly happy and comfortable in the skin that they are already in. Respect that fact. Because that is what being a true friend and loved one is all about. Your journey was exactly that, your journey. Not there's. Respect the differences and enjoy the love that you already have in the relationship, for what it is already worth.

> *"The pain and hurt from your past,*
>
> *Has nothing to do with the hope and promise,*
>
> *Of your future.*
>
> *Leave yourself open to love,*
>
> *Despite the pain you've survived.*
>
> *And you will be able to receive*
>
> *More than you ever even knew existed."*

Many people have a nasty habit of attributing their current circumstances to the countless bad experiences and traumas they have managed to survive from years ago. And they use those bad experiences from the past, as their excuse for not being able to do all that they believe they are actually called to do now, in the present. They utilize those bad experiences as justification to substantiate their fears and abandon all hope of ever pursuing their passions for fear of reliving the pain of failure. For lack of belief within themselves, in their own dreams. They've come to the conclusion that it's easier to never even try, then to try and to fail or be embarrassed. They don't want to deal with the possibility of disappointment. Better not to even try at all, then to try and fail. That is there logic. And their downfall. This pertains to goals as well as relationships.

If you allow the past to dictate the possibilities in your future, you will never have a future to speak of. Each day that you live and breathe you add onto your life's experience. You learn, you grow, and you evolve. You become stronger, wiser and more confident as you are able to integrate and employ your new-found knowledge and skills into your everyday life. So, you find that as time passes, something that was impossible for you to do a year ago, became possible after working at it for a few weeks. Then after a month or two you became proficient at it. After 6 months it became easy for you to handle without much effort at all. And now after a year, you are able to perform the task without even thinking about it. But if you "BRAINWASH" yourself to believe that you cannot do something more, or achieving something more, or accomplish something more, because of something you experienced years, decades in the past, you are cutting yourself off from any hope of ever doing more or being more than who and what you were, way back when you first experienced that bad thing all those years ago.

Nick Moore

Stop putting limitations on your own mind. We are limitless beings with an unlimited capacity for EVERYTHING. The only thing that stands between you and your ability to do whatever it is that your heart is aching to do, is the effort that you are, or are not willing to put into pursuing that desire. Your passion is your passion for a reason. And like it or not, it is a part of who and what you are. To deny it, is to deny yourself.

The heart and the mind, though separate entities, together comprise our living soul. And because of that, they are undeniably connected. So, when the mind begins to validate a legitimate reason as to why your being cannot have something that your soul is longing for, you have internal grief and conflict. Resolution for that grief and conflict is simple, instead of always leaning more to the side of fear, and allowing your mind to begin formulating that list of negatives against your heart's desire, get proactive and immediately get your hands on a pen and a piece of paper and start constructing a literal physical list of what you need to make that desire a reality.

Things in your life are as real and as important as you allow them to be. Make a list. And then make that list a priority. And you can make that dream or desire a reality. It's a choice. A decision. A commitment.

"We were not born,

To sit quietly in the dark,

Never Too Late

But to sing, to dance, to laugh and cry,

And to learn what it means to love.

Live your life out loud!"

I can't stress this one enough. Life is not all about WORK! WORK! WORK! What is the point of it all if you are not in a position to live, love and laugh as often as possible?

It is very easy to get so caught up in your daily routine of working, and to deal with your various responsibilities, that you lose sight of the other aspects of life. You have to be mindful to maintain a healthy balance in every area of your life. You have worked hard to achieve whatever level of success you now enjoy, you should play equally as hard. We work in order to sustain our livelihood, but to "LIVE LIFE" is to experience it in all of its various forms, colors and sensations!

Truly living your life means more than the making it through your daily or weekly work routine in order to meet your responsibilities. And being able to live in the moment is just as important as doing what is necessary to prepare for your future. There is a time and a place for everything under the sun. And that includes the ability to live, love and laugh! Make the time to smell the roses and to enjoy your friends and family. The moments shared with them is what helps you to keep your own situation in its proper perspective.

You also want to take some time just for you. Time to be still. Time to be alone with your own thoughts. Making the time for your own self-evaluations are key to keeping track of your own progress and peace of mind.

Remember, success is measured by more than just what you have sitting in your bank account. It's measured by love. By friends and family. By invitations to parties and trips. It's measured by your ability to feel good about who you are in the light of day while in the company of the people who matter most. No masks, no disguises or fronts. Your view of how others perceive you is a powerful motivator. It can be rewarding. Or it can be damning. However, no one's view of you, is more important than your own.

"Next level thinking,

Will force you to do next level work.

And it will yield those next level results,

That will give you that next level life,

That you want and deserve.

If you want and extraordinary life,

You need to be willing to do,

Some extraordinary work/things."

Never Too Late

Everyone wants to mimic the lifestyle that they see portrayed by their favorite stars. They want to be able to travel to exotic locations and enjoy the finer things in life, but none of them are putting forth the work or effort that their favorite stars have had to put in, in order for them to reach their level of success. People who live that lifestyle are able to do so because of what they have invested in themselves. So the question becomes; What are you willing to invest in yourself?

At the very beginning of this book it was explained that the best way to get from where you are to where you want to be is to sit down and map out what you need to accomplish to get you to your goal. Take the time to do the research in order to find out what those steps are, write them down in a list format so that you can check them off one by one as you complete each step. That is the kind of dedication that it takes to live that kind of life.

For you to make it to the peak of your abilities and prowess and put out the best version of "YOU" that can be put out there, you need to be committed to doing the work that needs to be done to get you there. No one can do it for you. So, if your goal is to be a movie star, or a singer or a writer, a construction worker, or to be a business owner, or to be the best parent that you can be, or the best mate or spouse, to be a better contributor, a better provider, find out what steps you need to take to elevate you to your next level of success and get to work. Yes, it is hard work, but that is why the rewards are bigger. Why the pay is better.

Why the living is finer. And the air a little sweeter. Nothing worth having is ever very easily attained. (Unless you were born with a trust fund or given an inheritance or hit the lottery for a major jackpot!)

"The reason God gave us all a voice,

Is because WE ALL have something important to say.

And WE ALL have the right,

To say whatever that thing is.

Always speak your mind,

And speak it from your heart."

On more than one occasion you will find yourself in a position that will issue an edict form your very soul to do more than just sit quietly or stand idly by and say nothing. We initially get our moral compass from our parents as children, but as adults you begin to groom your own set of morals and understandings and beliefs in what you feel is "RIGHT VS. WRONG."

It can be something as simple as an idea that you want to contribute to your family or your at your job. It can be an injustice you see with your own eyes being carried out in the middle of the street. It can be an ongoing problem that you have taken note of in your community or church that you feel can be handled better. It can be a domestic issue with a neighbor abusing their children or their spouse. It can be seated emotions that you have for someone that you are attracted to. Whatever the case, you need to have the confidence and the freedom to act upon the things that you are feeling.

The whole point of linear thinking is for you to be able to identify the things that are important to you and then logically map out a plan of action to attain or resolve those things. After mapping it out a plan, physically go out and execute the plan. Each step being relevant to the next simply because there would be no reason for any of the steps to exist without the end result!

So, if you find that for whatever reason, something in you is being motivated to take action on something that you see or hear, if it commands your attention to the point of you needing to speak on it, then by speaking, you are already acting. Follow through. Because everything in this life is relevant and has value and is worthy of your respect and the respect of everyone else, regardless of their station or status in life. At the end of the day, we are all just human beings. Common courtesy and respect truly is all that separates us from the animals.

Acknowledge whatever it is that has been placed upon your heart and approach it with a clear logical mind. Speak your peace and speak it from the heart.

Nick Moore

"As a rule,

Every single day,

Consciously make the effort,

To try and be a better person today,

Than the person you were yesterday."

What will set you apart from the rest, is your never ending conscious decision to always try and be a better person today than you were the day before.

This takes a great deal of honesty with your own self. It requires a person to look at their own actions throughout their day and ask themselves; "Could I have handled that better than the way I handled it?" A lot of people simply do not have the capacity to do this because they don't want to do anything that makes their own lives any harder or more complicated than it already is. Most people are actually just lazy. And the easy answers, the quick fixes make life more pleasant for them. They have no desire to put forth the extra effort because the current dysfunction of their lives feels normal and has already been accepted for a very long time and they are comfortable with things exactly as they are.

Never Too Late

The improvement of one's life only comes with change. And the more you work at removing the negative aspects out of your life, the more room you make for more positive aspects. There is never room for both. In scenario's where you have both cohabitating, one always ends up cancelling out the other. That being the case, wisdom dictates that you take control of the situation and dictate for yourself what should stay and what should be discarded. It will greatly assist you in keeping the chaos down to a minimum while frequently rewarding you with the benefits that come with surrounding yourself with positive people, positive influences and positive energy.

The one thing you do not want to do however is find yourself in a state of denial. We all know people who frequently do things the wrong way and make mistakes and try to continue to push forward as though the consistent error that they are making is in fact right when they in fact already know that it is incorrect.

Pretending that mistakes or problems do not exist after you make them is a form of denial that is self-destructive. You can learn from them only AFTER you acknowledge them. And then you will find yourself in a position to correct them, thus correcting yourself. That's called growth. That's called maturity. That's called progress, THAT'S CALLED REAL LIFE. And that is what you are going to have to deal with if you want to honestly put yourself in a place of growth and improvement.

Nick Moore

Anyone who can look at themselves in the mirror and never see any room for improvement or growth only does themself an injustice. Life is a continual flow of growth and development. And if the world is in a constant state of change and growth and flux, then we are also.

"Most people fear change.

They fear that leaving their comfort zone,

Will put them at a disadvantage.

And for some, that disadvantage,

Is like the end of the world.

But change, like time, is inevitable.

Don't fear it, embrace it.

And then learn to thrive in it!"

Change is a natural part of life. Everything that exists within our eco-system has been designed to change. Change is growth. Change is evolution. It is time gathering unto itself the accumulated knowledge and experience of its lifespan. Constantly making new adjustments to accommodate the new additions, information and growth. Nothing that exists remains unchanged. With that understanding in mind, it is safe for me to say that being fearful of "CHANGE" is foolish and a waste of time, simply because change is inevitable. Wisdom dictates that the intelligent thing to do would be to adapt to whatever the change is. Then learn all you can learn about the change so that you can maneuver yourself into a position to either benefit from it, or at the very least, position yourself in a place of safety so that you won't be in the path of any possible harmful fallout.

In any scenario where you know that there are certain elements that are inevitable, you should always strive to embrace the natural order of things. And that means embracing the changes. If you are able to embrace and adapt to the changes, then when they come you will be unfazed by the changes that take effect. And if the changes are something that is predictable, you will be able to gauge what times are the most opportune or beneficial for you. There is always an upside to any scenario. You just have to want to see it. And if you are wise, figure out how to use it to your advantage. Knowledge is power and power is leverage and leverage is a tool that can be used for anything that suits your needs. Just food for thought.

"Just because you gave up

On your dreams,

Don't expect me,

To give up on mine!

There is an old adage that says: "Misery loves company." That is in fact the truth. And you will find that there will be people in your circle who like you have been striving towards their own goals and dreams, but unlike you, were ill prepared and less determined than you. The majority of people have a low tolerance for failure. And after falling on their face once or twice, quickly come to the conclusion that; "It simply wasn't meant to be." And they immediately give up on their passion. Mentally convincing themselves that they gave it their best shot and that God or a higher power must want their lives to go in a completely different direction than the one they have been travelling.

Oprah Winfrey was fired from her first job because she was deemed "UNFIT FOR TV." Michael Jordan, arguably the greatest basketball player of all time, missed more than 9,000 shots in his career. He's lost almost 300 games. 26 times he was given the ball, trusted to make the winning shot and actually missed it. In his own words: "I've failed over and over and over again in my life, and that is why I succeed!"

Failure is never a reason to quit. If anything it should only strengthen your resolve to figure out what you missed or what went wrong so that you can go back and kick it in the proverbial backside! There is an upside to failing. You get a first hand lesson on what does and does not work. And you are now armed with new information to help you in your endeavor. Failing is nothing more than a stepping stone towards your success. Whether you fail one time or one hundred times, you have not truly failed unless you have quit! And quitting is never an option.

That being said, you need to be able to silence your naysayers. Don't even give them the opportunity to get under your skin with their negativity. Because their words can be like poisonous venom, and will spread throughout your mind and heart and soul, killing your dreams from the inside out if you allow it. In this instance what you are experiencing is a form of transference. They are sharing their own disappointment, their own sense of defeat from their failed attempts at pursuing their dreams, with you. There is your misery seeking your company.

DO NOT ALLOW THIS

UNDER ANY CIRCUMSTANCE!

Anyone that wants to abandon their own dreams for whatever reason that is their own personal demon that they themselves will have to figure out and deal with on their own one day. Your focus has to be on getting back up on that horse and riding it down into the ground if need be, to the glorious victory of achieving your soul's passion. Period. No matter how many times it takes. You haven't lost anything unless you quit trying or striving. Again, quitting is NOT an option.

Nick Moore

"Stop seeking the approval of others.

There are only two opinions

That matter at all, ...

Yours and Gods."

Most people do not like to admit this, but the truth is that the opinions of others has great influence on the minds and hearts of a great many people. Subconsciously we all want to be liked. There is no one who does not enjoy praise when it is being giving to them. But when it comes to matters of the heart, you will quickly find that a lot of the time, you are sitting in a class by yourself. Something in you alone sees the value in whatever it is that has enthralled your heart. And it won't really dawn on you until you share your new-found interest with those around you. The response you are likely to get from those around you will be a dazed look in their eye and a question in the form of a single word;

"Why?"

Trying to explain it is a wasted endeavor. They cannot share in your excitement because they cannot share in your passion. They can only wish you the best and be happy that you are happy, but they will never really actually "get it." So why is it so important to impress them or seek their approval when they don't even really care like you do?

Listen, your passion is more than just some random interest that has your attention for the moment. From before you were born your passion was embedded within the essence of your soul which is why it resonates so deeply within you once you are able to identify what it is that you are passionate about. It's a personal mission that is given to you, for you alone to acknowledge and appreciate. If you really want others to appreciate it like you do, then let your passion for whatever it is, drive you to elevate it to the next step in its evolutionary journey. People love when someone is able to elevate something to an art form. Make it into something so beautiful, that you force the whole world to stop and take notice. That is what your talent, or your passion for whatever it is, has the power and potential to do. People who do this become superstars. Or world famous, world renowned. Other than that, you owe no one any explanation for anything. You are accountable to only two people in the whole of the Universe. Yourself and God. The end.

"In the cold void that was my life,

Her love was the substance

That gave me shape and form.

It filled me with a power

And a purpose I had never known.

Nick Moore

Our love evolved into a passion

That ignited our very beings and

Became a cosmic force that

Enveloped our souls and

Propelled our spirits to a place

Beyond space and time."

This book is about making your passion your life. But there is more than one kind of passion. There is the passion in which the text within these pages has covered in abundance and then there is the kind of passion that we as human beings have for each other. And by passion for each other, I do not mean just the sexual aspects. I am very specifically speaking about the passion that is shared between two people who are indeed "IN LOVE" with each other.

Make no mistake about this; if you are currently in a relationship or married and you are also a person who is actively pursuing their passion, both of these passions directly affect each other. And depending on where you and your mate are mentally and emotionally, it has the potential to either enhance your relationship or to destroy it.

This is the place that makes and breaks relationships. Especially when you are talking about people with ambitions. Before we can get into any specifics, we need to establish a definition for what true love actually is.

In a marriage or a romantic relationship where both parties are genuinely "IN LOVE" there are some very specific characteristics that you can use to identify and indeed establish a factual foundation for love in your relationship.

It doesn't matter what culture or what country you hail from, love is universally the same for us all. Love in its purest form is called "SACRIFICE." So, when you finally find yourself in a relationship where the welfare and wellbeing of the other person is more important to you than your own, then you are officially there.

Love is patience and kindness and the seeds that it sows leaves you with a craving to always be in the presence of the one you love. "LOVE" means being able to accept somebody for who they are and not for who you want them to be, or for who you think they can be, or for who you want to try and mold them into being. Their choices and their path is what shaped them into the person that you fell in love with. What SHOULD happen is that each person in the relationship should be able to help the other with the nurturing of their own individual growth. Respecting each other's differences and supporting each other's decisions, dreams and ambitions should be expected and encouraged. In a lot of instances however, that IS NOT what happens at all.

Nick Moore

If you happen to have the misfortune of being in a relationship or marriage with a mate who is needy and unsupportive of your passion, meaning that he or she is unable to see your vision or relate to your need to pursue it, then you now have a different kind of obstacle to overcome. It is very important for your mate to be onboard with you in your endeavors. Their motivation and support can be the thing that sustains you when you hit those low spots, and the accomplishment of your dreams is made even sweeter when you are able to share in it together. What you DO NOT want, is for your mate to view your passion as something that they are now being forced to compete with for your time. This actually happens more often than most people would believe`. The more emotionally involved you are, the more your mate values the time that is spent with you. Especially if you two already have an established routine. Once you begin to actively pursue your passion, that routine is going to change drastically. For you to do what needs to be done in the pursuit of mastering your skills, it will take time, energy and focus. And that is time and energy and focus that you are NOT giving to your significant other. Every success story that I am familiar with has some common denominators in them. The biggest one is that they all were dedicated to a fault to do whatever it took to earn their degrees, hone their skills, get as much experience as they could, work on projects after hours, after work, meaning they had very little free time. Now if your mate is committed to riding this out with you, training with you, or working with you in any capacity to help spur you on and aid you in achieving your goal. (Actually making YOUR goal or passion, the goal or passion of you both as a couple), then wonderful! It will strengthen the relationship between you. And you are still actually spending time together as you strive together to get whatever needs to be done out of the way.

"That will not be the case however,

if they have made it clear that they are not with you

and do not support your decision to pursue your dreams."

First you will have to deal with the "REVERSE PSYCHOLOGY" in the form of guilt trips. They will accuse you of not really loving them. They will insist that you have changed. That you are putting something else before the love that you share. And you will feel pressured into having to make a decision between your current relationship or the continued pursuit of your dreams. And this is the worst kind of stress imaginable.

The number of people who have given up on their dreams because of love or a relationship, is simply staggering. We seem to have accepted as a fundamental truth, that it has to be one or the other, which is absolute non-sense. There is absolutely NO reason why you cannot have BOTH. And now for the hard part:

"If you have a mate that is placing you in the position of having to choose between your life's passion or your relationship; LOSE THE RELATIONSHIP AND CHASE YOUR DREAM!"

Nothing is worse than spending a lifetime angry at yourself and your mate for giving up on your passion, your vision, the very thing that you believe you were put on this planet to do. And even if you convince yourself that you made the right decision by not pursuing your passion or your dreams, it will haunt you. And every time you see someone else doing what you always wanted to do, it will sting. It will hurt. And that sense of regret simply never goes away.

I can tell you with all confidence and certainty that if you do indeed have a mate that is insisting that you give up on the things that matter most to you, that they are not the person you were meant to be with. And that at best, the relationship is dysfunctional and will bring you more misery than joy.

"How can I make such a huge blanket statement

Like that without even knowing the people

I'm talking about?"

Simple, I understand the fundamental dynamics and workings of both a functional and a dysfunctional relationship. And I can tell you without any inclination of a doubt, that anyone in a relationship with a mate who does not encourage them, or does not help to foster their ambition or aid in their endeavors to better themselves, for their own selfish reasons, is participating in a relationship that has no future and no hope of sustaining any lasting joy or peace. One sided relationships NEVER do.

Relationships that are able to stand the test of time consist of people who have each other's backs. They support each other's decisions. And if it's important one of them, it becomes important to the both of them by default. A relationship, though a partnership, is a lot like a team. And there is no "I" in the word "team."

Now, I am not suggesting that the feelings that the two of you obviously feel are not real. I am merely saying that if you are going to be in a relationship with ANYONE, it needs to be someone who understands that you are a man or a woman with goals and ambitions and a dream. And that though you do indeed love them, you are still your own individual person. You already had your own identity long before they ever came along. Becoming a willing participant in a relationship does not mean that your identity as an individual has suddenly gone away. You are still that same person with those same wants and needs, dreams and desires. And at the very least, if they can't get on board with that, they need not do or say anything to hinder you from you pursuing your endeavor. If they truly love you, they have no choice but to agree. If they out right disagree, you need to nip that in the bud right there on the spot before emotions get any deeper or either of you waste any more time, energy or money.

> *"Dear Reader,*
>
> ***The world and your life,***
>
> ***Is what you choose to make of it.***
>
> ***You are responsible***
>
> ***For your own happiness!***

For my readers who are from the younger generation, this message is specifically for you, (and anyone else who's foot inadvertently happens to also fit this same shoe). In this most recent decade our civilization has seen a great many advances in our technology which has directly impacted the family dynamic. Consequently, life has been made easier, more convenient and information is much more accessible. Personally, in my opinion, if you are reading this book, I think that it shows a depth of character that belies your years. And to your credit, I have to assume that your reading of this material can only mean that you have determined within yourself to be more than what you already are. Because you believe that you are called to be more. For you I issue these words of encouragement;

Never Too Late

Between your boyfriend/girlfriend scenarios, drama with your parents, peer pressure and your own hormones, you have a list of obstacles that most adults no longer have to deal with. Staying the course is actually going to be harder for you. But you can do it.

What you want to do is to establish yourself your own routine that will allow you to encompass everything you need to do within the day. Write it down on paper and then post it in plain sight like on the refrigerator or your wall. Follow it religiously. No exceptions. No exceptions. No exceptions.

You are bound to make your fair share of mistakes. SO WHAT? That is what life is. We live, we make mistakes, we learn from those mistakes, and then we push right on through to do it again, hopefully learning each time we make whatever mistakes we made so that we do not make the same identical mistakes again. That is called getting experience. That is called paying your dues. That is called "LIFE." But whatever you do, DO NOT GIVE UP ON YOUR DREAMS. Whatever you do, DO NOT STOP PURSUING YOUR PASSION. Whatever you do, DON'T YOU EVER QUIT!!!

For those of us who have embraced this in our latter years, we've had to learn our lesson the hard way. And though we are able to enjoy the fruits of our labor now, it's hard to not acknowledge the fact that life could have been this good 20 years earlier if we had only did then what we are doing now.

Nick Moore

Your blessing is that you are being put on your path at the earliest possible point of your life. The earlier that you are able to come into the embracing and the mastering of your passion, the more time you have to enjoy the fruits of your labor. The longer it takes you to get your stuff together, the less time you have to enjoy it. Remember, from the moment that we are born, we are already growing old and nearing our time for departure from this world. Before you leave this earth, leave your mark upon it. Leave a legacy behind for others to benefit from. Whether that be a family home that you build, a business that you leave to your children, an invention you create that blesses the rest of the world, and inheritance for family members, creating an organization for the needy, a charity, a club, a word of encouragement. You make it your business to leave something behind for the ones that you are leaving behind. Because in case you haven't figured it out by this stage of the book, there is one common denominator that people's individual passions share; They will always, in some way, touch the lives or the hearts or the pockets of others. Your blessing blesses you, because in some way, it will always bless others. So you see, believe it or not, you pursuing your dreams, allows others to pursue theirs. When you look at it that way, nothing about that sounds selfish at all.

"You haven't failed,

Until you have decided to give up.

Make it up in your mind NOW,

Never Too Late

That failure is "NOT" an option.

Because giving up is never an option."

This is easily the most redundant phrase you will find in my book. And as redundant as it has been, it still has not been emphasized enough. I have friends and colleagues who like me have figured out the importance and significance in going back to reclaim our passions and dreams and to see them to fruition. In fact it was working with so many other men and women over the age of 50 that inspired me to write this book. It is exciting to see so many people reawaken the fire that once lived inside of them. And the transformation is truly something to behold. As a professional life coach I've worked with hundreds of men and women and walked with them throughout their journey. Some as short as 6 months, some as long as 6 years. And the list of changes that one goes through can be traumatic in itself. But if it's important to you, then it's important to me.

Clearly, the one thing that all of my clients said was that they wish that they had stayed with this back when they were first set on fire about whatever their particular passion is. There is a keen sense of accomplishment for finally attaining whatever their individual goals were. There was also a keen sense of loss for all of the years wasted that they feel like they should have still been doing it. The all echo the same words; "Man, if I had stayed on top of this from back when I first fell in love with this, do you realize how far along I would be?" – Indeed. They would be masters. Authorities in their fields. Capable of naming their own price for any service they did. It's a bittersweet experience. And it's one that no one has to experience if you just remember that YOU DON'T HAVE TO QUIT. Not now, not ever.

No matter what your interest is, in today's world, there are a myriad of ways to surround yourself with the people and the positive support you need to keep you focused on your grind and seeing your dreams to fruition. There are support groups and fraternities, tutors, clubs, family, friends, and mates. If you have somehow managed to find yourself in an environment that is hostile towards the life of your dream or passion, simply leave. There are too many things that you have working in your favor, for you to choose or have to settle for the route that forces you to abandon the things that mean the most to you.

Don't give up and do not quit. Because if you do, the truth of the matter is, you're not really giving up on your dream or your passion.... you're giving up on YOU. And no matter who you are or where you are from, nothing about quitting, can ever amount to anything good.

In closing, I leave you with the most important piece of information and advice that I have ever given anyone. There is a scripture in the bible that reminds me daily of just how much power we as individual souls truly have. Proverbs 18:21 says; "Death and life are in the power of the tongue...." It reminds me that we have the power to speak into

Never Too Late

existence the things that we want in our lives. You can look at it as another form of "POSITIVE REINFORCEMENT." When we speak things out loud, like in the mantras, we are consciously gearing our minds in a very specific direction in order to complete a very specific task. Make no mistake about this, everything in your life is a choice. You do not have to remain a victim of your own circumstances. If you are unhappy with ANY aspect of your life, you have the ability to STOP what you are doing, and to literally start CONSTRUCTING a whole new life for yourself. And you can start by speaking it into existence. It's very important to say out loud, all of the things that you desire. It gives your thoughts and feelings form and weight. Helps to make them more tangible to the mind and therefore easier to focus on as a goal.

That being said, you want to be mindful about what it is you say when you are speaking in terms of you and your future, your ability to succeed. Speak favor unto yourself. Speak prosperity. We live in a Universe that is based on the laws of cause and effect. And for those of you who believe in it, Karma as well. If you surround yourself with good people and do good work and have good intentions, then "GOOD THINGS" is what you can expect. When you put good out into the universe, then goodness is all the universe has to send back to you… times three!

Remember the rules to mapping out your plan. Start your mapping by verbally speaking it out loud. Make it real within your own mind.

Nick Moore

Envision yourself within each step. Start mentally programming your mind as accepting this truth as already in the works. Remember, if you can conceive it, you can achieve it. Speaking a thing out loud makes it easier to mentally envision it. Mentally envisioning it makes it easier to move towards and makes you more accepting and mentally prepared for the steps when they come. You can never be too prepared. So, speak victory, speak achievement, speak life, love and prosperity over your own life. Because the best encouragement you will ever receive, will be from YOURSELF. You. The one who has to do the actual work and endure what must be endured during your journey. You will be giving up a great deal of yourself, but the life that you are given for accomplishing your goals makes it all worthwhile.

Congratulations on taking the first steps towards pursuing your passion. I bid you a safe and successful journey. And I look forward to your stories, comments and questions. Peace love and blessings to you all.

- Nick Moore

ABOUT THE AUTHOR

Nick Moore was born in Oklahoma City, Oklahoma, to his parents; Katherine Ford and Sanders Moore Jr., by age 3 he was adopted by his grandparents; Mary Jo Moore (May Jo) Sanders Moore Sr., who raised him to be the man that he would become today. He raised two beautiful children, in a 16 year-long marriage, with his ex-wife Zinnia, a son, Jordan Michael Moore and a daughter, Kiara Nicole Moore. Since then, Nick has remarried, and together with his current wife, the beautiful and loving Dawn Moore, they are now raising his step-children; Draven and Deija.

Nick's love for the children and for family comes from his own experiences with family and the obstacles they had to face in having to create opportunities where none had previously existed. Nick's

Nick Moore

Grandfather, Sanders Moore Sr., met and fell in love with Nick's grandmother, Mary Jo Moore, on the cotton fields of Detroit, Texas. At the time she was pregnant with Nick's father; Sanders Moore Jr. In a desperate attempt to secure their love, his grandfather literally stole his wife, Mary Jo, off of that cotton field, jumped into his car and drove as far as they could until they ran out of gas in Wichita Falls, Texas, where they ultimately settled. His grandfather took on the job of working on the property of a wealthy land owner, and raised his family there. He and his wife were living examples to Nick of what it means to be family, and what it means to conquer adversity. That love, and those lessons were deeply engrained into the mind and heart of Nick, who went on to extend that love and those lessons to others through his work in these various organizations and foundations.

There was no scenario in which Nick could not find a way to turn a negative situation into a positive opportunity. Once, as a child, Nick had gotten in trouble for breaking the rules, his grandfather decided that his punishment would be to dig up the backyard with nothing but a shovel and a hoe. Instead of wallowing in self-pity, Nick took advantage of the situation, by digging up the yard and planting a garden which grew a wonderful crop of vegetables that he would later harvest and sell to the Senior Citizens Community that he grew up in with his grandparents. It was his grandmother who had taught him how to plant and to fish. Curious as a child, whenever they would visit the country, he would always ask questions about every little thing he would see.

Like; "What's in the water?" And his grandmother would do more than just give him a verbal answer. She would tell him;

"Fish and snakes and turtles, all kinds of life."

Then she got him a cane pole with some string and a hook and a can of worms so that he could discover for himself, what was in the water as a fisherman. They taught him the value of live experiences. And how every little thing was connected to everything else, big and small.

A gifted athlete, Nick was offered several athletic scholarships in both football and basketball, ultimately signing a football scholarship with Arizona State University. He also has an Associate's Degree in Sociology from Scottsdale and Glendale Community Colleges. That experience would take him to France where he played professional basketball on a tour team that did fundraising to build public parks in Europe for kids. After his stint in Europe he was offered the opportunity to play for the world-famous Harlem Globetrotters. He trained with them for five months awaiting the retirement of the player whom he was to replace, but that player had decided that he would stay in the game a few years longer. Making the position he was to take, no longer available. Not willing to take a less pay or a different position, Nick returned home to work on his family and decide on the next chapter of his life. He has always had a passion for helping the youth to reach their maximum potential, so Nick begins a one-man crusade to reach out to troubled teens and encourage them to stay in school and to keep reaching for their dreams, despite the obstacles standing in their way. He was instrumental in helping to organize the Phoenix Suns "Nite Hoops Foundation" as an Assistant Director.

Nick started the "Motivate The Children, Youth Foundation" in which he toured and did assemblies, clinics, halftime shows, parent presentations, throughout several states, Arizona, New Mexico, Utah, Colorado, Texas, Oklahoma, Nevada and California touching the lives of over 250,000 students since 1994. The feedback from the kids themselves has been incredible. It is confirmation that the work he is doing is needed and making a difference.

Nick Moore is also the founder and owner of "SMALL TOWN ATHLETES." An organization that specializes in working with kids who want to train to push their athletic ability to its maximum potential, encouraging student athletes in small towns to pursue their dreams and set goals to be successful athletes or students.

The main focus is fitness and dedication in the classroom and in whichever sport they are competing in! Teaching and motivating parents on how to get more involved in their child's college recruiting process. He has been successful in helping many of these young adults attain both athletic and academic scholarships for college. He is based out of Wichita Falls, Texas, where he continues to make a home with his wife Dawn. For contact or booking info as a motivational speaker

Never Too Late

for your company, organization, colleges, school, or league, please contact him at:

Website: www.smalltownathletes.com

Email: athletesgoingtocollege@gmail.com

motivatethechildren@yahoo.com

Or send a letter to:

Small Town Athletes
P.O. Box 215
Wichita Falls, TX 76306

Nick Moore

Never Too Late

Nick Moore

Never Too Late

Nick Moore

Never Too Late

Nick Moore

Never Too Late

Nick Moore

Never Too Late

Nick Moore

Never Too Late

Nick Moore

Never Too Late

1998 Harlem Globetrotters.

Nick Moore

No DAys
off !!
Get better
daily!!